£1·50

D014532

Critical Guides to Spanish Texts

23 Pérez Galdós: Miau

Critical Guides to Spanish Texts

EDITED BY J. E. VAREY AND A. D. DEYERMOND

PÉREZ GALDÓS

Miau

Eamonn Rodgers

Lecturer in Spanish,
Trinity College, Dublin

Grant & Cutler Ltd *in association with*
Tamesis Books Ltd 1978

ISBN 0 7293 0059 5

I.S.B.N. 84-399-8416-2
DEPÓSITO LEGAL: V. 1.689 - 1978

Printed in Spain by
Artes Gráficas Soler, S. A. - Jávea, 28 - Valencia (8)
for
GRANT AND CUTLER LTD
11 BUCKINGHAM STREET, LONDON, W.C.2.

Contents

Contents

References

EXCEPT where otherwise indicated, references to Galdós's writings are to the six-volume Aguilar edition of the *Obras completas*. Quotations from *Miau* are taken from the edition by Robert J. Weber (Barcelona: Labor, 1973), which is based on the first edition of 1888. References to the Weber edition precede those to Volume V of the Aguilar *Obras completas*, in parentheses after each quotation. The Weber edition also includes Galdós's manuscript of a primitive version of *Miau*, which Weber calls Alpha, Beta being the revised version which formed the basis for the printed text. Page references to Alpha are to the Weber volume.

The italic figures in parentheses refer to numbered items in the Bibliographical Note; the italic figure is followed by a page reference.

CHAPTER I

Galdós and the Rhetoric of Fiction

El estilo es la mentira. La verdad mira y calla (*Tormento*,
Chapter 12).

FOR many critics, the principal merit of Galdós's novels is that they give a detailed and authentic picture of middle-class Madrid in the last quarter of the nineteenth century. 'We know,' says J. M. Cohen, the translator of the Penguin edition of *Miau*, 'the streets and shops they [i.e., Galdós's characters] frequented, the churches into which they slipped for a moment's prayer, the courtyards they crossed to visit a neighbour.' Cohen is here articulating a critical commonplace which is widespread even in books and articles written by and for specialist students of Galdós. José F. Montesinos's three-volume study of the author is full of asides drawing attention to the historical and socio-logical accuracy of many of Galdós's characterizations. True, he does admit that 'el sociólogo está siempre asistido por un incom-parable artista' (4, vol. II, p. 145), but he sees the artist side of Galdós as ancillary to his sociological activity, giving colour and vividness to his descriptions of Madrid. Thus he declares that in *El Doctor Centeno*, 'todo el relato de lo que pasa en aquel espan-toso verano de 1864... es de lo mejor que el novelista había hecho hasta entonces y lo que da la medida de su sentido de la novela, arte esencialmente descriptivo, aun cuando narre' (II, 92).

Now it is, of course, undeniable that Galdós's novels, like all those written in the realist mode, are constructed out of accurately observed detail from the world around him. The realist novel seeks to say something about the ordinary everyday concerns which author and readers share. A realist novel is avowedly an invented story, a description of a fictional world, but this fictional world bears a sufficiently strong resemblance to the world in which the readers actually live to enable them to take the novel as relevant to their situation. It does not, however, follow that this resemblance to real life is the only important thing about the realist novel, or that the novelist's role is to be reduced to that of a mere transcriber. The thrust of Montesinos's approach, and that of very many academic critics, is to minimize the importance of the author's activity in selecting and arranging his material so as to affect the reader's perceptions in various ways. Some critics, indeed, would even attempt to deny the author's right to choose those aspects of contemporary life which he wishes to include in his novel: there are in print two substantial studies of Galdós which take him to task for leaving out aspects of Restoration life. [1]

It is important to understand why the approach I have described continues to exercise such a powerful influence. As Harry Levin reminded us in *The Gates of Horn* (New York, 1966), 'etymologically, realism is thing-ism' (p. 34). The realist mode in fiction is associated, in the minds of most readers, with the depiction of things which have objective reality, whether material objects or human figures, rather than with the transmission of subjective attitudes and perspectives. When, by contrast, we read Unamuno's *nivolas*, Joyce's *Finnegans Wake*, or the last chapter of Goytisolo's *Señas de identidad*, it is much more obvious to us that literary language is being deliberately manipulated for emotional or aesthetic effect. The realist novel, on the other hand, seems at first glance more straightforward. We are, it seems, being offered a credible story, involving descriptions of places and situations we can recognize from our own experience, and humanly typical characters with whom we can identify. Furthermore, the repeated assertions of realist writers that their novels were truer to life than those of their romantic predecessors seem to warrant our taking realist fiction at its own evaluation.

The course of the critical debate on *Miau* over the last twenty years pays eloquent testimony to the strength of this tendency to respond to realistic fiction by involving oneself personally in the fortunes and misfortunes of the characters. Most critical

[1] Antonio Regalado García, *Benito Pérez Galdós y la novela histórica española* (Madrid, 1966), p. 197; Francisco Pérez Gutiérrez, *El problema religioso en la Generación de 1868* (Madrid, 1975), p. 224.

approaches to the novel have concentrated on Villaamil's unemployment and his reaction to it, and have treated this issue
largely in isolation from the other blocks of human experience
which make up *Miau*. Furthermore, the presentation of Villaamil
has been discussed all too frequently in terms of the justice or
injustice of his dismissal from the public service, and the discussion has been conducted very often from standpoints much
more appropriate to moral choices in real life than to the eluci-
dation of literary texts. 'The modern reader,' declares A. A. Parker, '... should not forget that he too would clamour, if not to
heaven, at least to every Court of Appeal against such treatment' (*14*, 17).

This remark betrays an assumption, which Professor Parker
shares with many other critics, that Galdós's intention was to
make us put ourselves in Villaamil's place and identify with his
sufferings. If this assumption were correct, then *Miau* would be
just another novel of the kind which invites the reader to experience the excitement, fear, relief, sadness or joy that the events
depicted would evoke in us were they actually witnessed in
real life. It is my contention in this study, however, that *Miau*
is the sort of serious work of literary creation which demands
a highly complex and discerning set of responses. For all its
cultivation of verisimilitude, it is above all a highly sophisticated
linguistic artefact. The case for this view needs to be made,
and I shall try to argue it in the succeeding chapters. But
it seems safe enough to assume from the outset that the material
contained in *Miau* is not a purely factual description of a piece
of historical or social reality, but has been deliberately selected
and arranged so as to persuade the reader to perceive it in a
certain way.

Galdós, like any other novelist, evolved and perfected suitable
techniques of presentation only by a process of trial and error
extending over a long period of time. Nevertheless, he appears
to have been keenly aware from the outset of his career of the
powerful attractions exercised over the minds of readers by the
products of the literary imagination. The temptation to enter
into the fictional world as if it were the real one is always very
strong; Galdós himself once confessed to having been an avid
reader of the historical romances of Fernández y González. *La*

sombra, probably written about 1866, has usually been interpreted by critics as a fascinating exercise in depth psychology: Anselmo's anxieties about his wife's supposed infidelity induce hallucinations, to the point where he imagines that the figure of Paris steps out of a painting of Paris and Helen which hangs in his house. To Anselmo's diseased perception, the figure seems to acquire speech and movement and threatens to become his rival for the affections of his wife Elena. What is often overlooked, however, is that this improbable tale is told by Anselmo to a listener, who progresses from disbelief to amused tolerance, and then to keen interest, as the story takes hold of his imagination. This interlocutor retains a desire to find a rational explanation for these strange events, and later he assists Anselmo in working out a logical analysis of the experience, which accounts satisfactorily for all its elements. Even after everything has been rationalized, however, he can still momentarily feel the urge to ask Anselmo 'si la figura de Paris había vuelto a presentarse en el lienzo, como parecía natural' (IV, 227b). In the end he does not put this question, not because it is manifestly absurd, but because 'el caso no merecía la pena'. In other words, this sceptical, hard-headed rationalist has entered so fully into the spirit of Anselmo's tale that he can, even momentarily, accept as possible what is easily the most fantastic element of all.

Another early short story, *La novela en el tranvía* (1871), treats the same issue in a more humorous vein. The narrator, crossing Madrid in a tram, blends snatches of overheard conversation about actual crimes with elements from his dreams and memories of his reading of sensational novels to the point where his entire perception of the reality around him becomes distorted. In the end, he leaps from the tram and sets off in pursuit of an innocent passer-by whom he is convinced has murdered a certain countess about whom he had read in a novel. The humour conceals a serious point. It is not only that fiction has once again shown its power to captivate the imagination, but that it does so all the more insidiously because it retains some connection with objective fact. The narrator's highly-coloured view of events is not wholly fabricated within his own mind, but is to a large extent an exaggerated version of incidents which are corroborated from the conversations he hears. There *are* murky love intrigues, tyrannical husbands, and mysterious deaths, even if these things do not occur in the highly dramatic way in which the narrator imagines them happening.

Galdós, in other words, is keenly aware not only of the capacity of the human imagination for invention, but of the deeply-rooted need to arrange experience into patterns. Faced with the necessity of making some sense of the formless surge of experience which daily impinges on the consciousness, human beings find it convenient to arrange life into a few simple and easily-understood categories. Complexities, ambiguities and grey areas are awkward. It is much easier to postulate a series of clear oppositions between good and bad characters, moral and immoral behaviour, justice and injustice, and so on. To this need the popular novel provides a ready-made answer. Galdós's description of the popular novel in his *Observaciones sobre la novela contemporánea en España* (1870) has often been quoted, but since it is particularly apposite to the present argument, one may perhaps be forgiven for repeating it:

> El público ha dicho: 'Quiero traidores pálidos y de mira-
> da siniestra, modistas angelicales, meretrices con aureola,
> duquesas averiadas, jorobados románticos, adulterios, extre-
> mos de amor y odio', y le han dado todo esto. (6, 118)

So seductive is this schematized view of the world, adds Galdós, that it soon becomes a substitute for reality itself:

> En todas las imaginaciones hay el recuerdo, la visión de
> una sociedad que hemos conocido en nuestras lecturas: y
> tan familiarizados estamos con ese mundo imaginario que
> se nos presenta casi siempre con todo el color y la fijeza
> de la realidad, por más que las innumerables figuras que
> lo constituyen no hayan existido jamás en la vida, ni los
> sucesos tengan semejanza ninguna con los que ocurren
> normalmente entre nosotros. (6, 118)

The last statement, that the events of the fictional world are totally unlike those of everyday life, needs to be interpreted: as we have seen, the turgid imaginings of the narrator of *La novela en el tranvía* are based on real events. What Galdós means is that the tone and rhythm of everyday life is much less intense than the life of the fictional world, that real life is not organized around dramatic polarizations between good and evil, and does not, on the whole, consist of cataclysmic events. The qualification is important, for if there were no points of contact between the real world and the world of popular fiction, it would be less easy for people to use the stereotyped patterns of popular fiction as models for the interpretation of their own existence.

This is why Galdós sees the influence of the popular novel as spiritually and morally deleterious. It is not that the popular novel is licentious, though Galdós shared the prevailing fastidiousness about some of the crudities of French naturalism. It is not even that immersion in the ideal world of the popular novel may lead one to neglect one's responsibilities in the real world. It is, rather, that we are tempted to refer our ordinary experience back to pre-existing literary models. The popular novel does not offer a totally false image of reality, but a misleading one, ultimately unsound, that is, but sufficiently like reality to make us accept it as reliable.

So seriously did Galdós regard this issue that he chose to make it one of the unifying concerns of almost his entire literary production. '¡Yo he leído mi propia historia tantas veces...!' says the protagonist of *La desheredada* (1881); and she goes on,

> Y ¿qué cosa hay más linda que cuando nos pintan una joven pobrecita, muy pobrecita, que vive en una guardilla y trabaja para mantenerse; y esa joven, que es bonita como los ángeles y, por supuesto, honrada, más honrada que los ángeles, llora mucho y padece porque unos pícaros la quieren infamar; y luego, en cierto día, se para una gran carretela en la puerta y sube una señora marquesa muy guapa, y va a la joven, y hablan y se explican, y lloran mucho las dos, viniendo a resultar que la muchacha es hija de la marquesa, que la tuvo de un cierto conde calavera? Por lo cual, de repente cambia de posición la niña, y habita palacios, y se casa con un joven que ya, en los tiempos de su pobreza, la pretendía y ella le amaba... (IV, 1011b)

A comparable summary of a sentimental novel is given at the beginning of *Tormento* by the hack writer, José Ido del Sagrario, whose mental equilibrium is shaky, to say the least. But the tendency to interpret life in accordance with literary stereo-types is not confined to vapid girls or half-mad old men. At another point in *Tormento*, Don Francisco Bringas, a stolid, prag-matic character if ever there was one, greets the news of the penniless Amparo's engagement to the wealthy Agustín with the remark, 'Esto se podría titular *El premio de la virtud*' (IV, 1521b). And when Agustín and Amparo are reconciled after their break,

> Agustín se acercó a la joven, y sobre la cabeza de ella puso su mano en actitud parecida a la de los sacerdotes de teatro cuando figuran atraer sobre algún virtuoso perso-naje, mártir, neófito o cosa semejante, las bendiciones del cielo. (IV, 1567a-b)

One could multiply examples, and as the last quotation sug-gests, not all of them would have to do with the popular novel. For the novel is only one, albeit the most obvious and influen-tial, of the models by which people seek to interpret their expe-rience in the way which most ministers to their assumptions, expectations, ambitions, or self-esteem, or enables them to evade confronting life as it really is. The protagonists of *Ángel Guerra* and *Halma* use religious idealism as a way of concealing from themselves their real ambitions and needs. As we shall see in the succeeding chapters, the world of administration fulfils a comparable function for Villaamil.

Now given that Galdós was so preoccupied with this issue, and wished to make his readers aware of it as a problem, it follows that he could not allow the reader to fall into the same trap as the characters. If the main point of most of Galdós's novels is the unwisdom of settling for the obvious, easy, conventionally-sanctioned view of things, the reader, if he is to see the point, has to be preserved somehow from becoming involved in the same process of error. To allow his reader the traditional liter-ary pleasures of identification with characters or involvement in situations would preclude that detachment necessary to enable him to see the ease with which human beings succumb to shallow and conventional ways of thinking. We therefore need to define very precisely what we mean when we say that Galdós's novels

contain characters 'just like ourselves'. Plainly, if characters in
fiction are too bizarre and untypical, we can dismiss their doings
as of no relevance to us. On the other hand, while recognizing
the likeness of the characters to the common run of humanity,
including ourselves, we need to stand far enough back from
them to take an objective and comprehensive view of their
strengths and weaknesses. If we identify with characters to the
point of uncritically taking their part, we shall be less alert to
the possible moral implications of the novel for our own behaviour.

Conscious as he was of the power of fiction over the imagination, Galdós was equally aware of the need to maintain strict
control over the distance between the reader and the world of
the novel. The scope of this study prohibits a full discussion of
the whole range of techniques whereby Galdós maintains aesthetic distance, and manipulates the reader into taking a more
complex and sophisticated view of everyday experience. But we
may here mention two, because they are probably the most
important: irony and analogy.

There are many kinds of irony, but here we need concern
ourselves only with what might be called the deflationary variety,
often known as Cervantine irony. That is to say that there is
a tone or use of language which implies that any solemn, heroic
or highly-dramatized view of reality is inappropriate, reality
being characteristically low-key, monochrome and prosaic. 'El
siglo prosaico' is a phrase which frequently occurs, not only in
the novels, but in many of Galdós's newspaper articles as well.
The following passage, from one of Galdós's contributions to
the Buenos Aires newspaper, *La Prensa*, sums up at once a
political philosophy and a theory of the novel:

> La medianía reina en todo, y los caracteres, cortados por
> el patrón corriente, parece que buscan la uniformidad.
> Huyeron los tiempos dramáticos, y las personas, como los
> hechos, parece que se informan en los moldes apacibles
> y rutinarios de la comedia de costumbres. [2]

[2] Benito Pérez Galdós, *Obras inéditas*, edited by Alberto Ghiraldo, Vol. I
(Madrid, 1923), p. 97.

This does not mean that Galdós is indifferent to or incapable of the representation of human tragedy. There can be few novels which convey a stronger sense of wasted and blighted lives than *Fortunata y Jacinta* (1886-7). Yet the tragedy is perceived by the reader with all the more immediacy because Galdós's dry, matter-of-fact style does not encourage us to take refuge in shallow emotional posturing. Galdós's dictum 'El estilo es la mentira. La verdad mira y calla' has a wide range of reference. It suggests a guiding principle not only for the novelist, but for the characters he creates, and also for the reader. That is to say that Galdós's ironic detachment enables us to be aware, without sacrificing any of our consciousness of human suffering, of the self-dramatization to which those who suffer are prone, and consequently of the inappropriateness of a facile, sentimental response on our part.

A convenient example of how this deflationary irony works in practice is provided by the description of the beggars in the opening chapter of *Misericordia* (1897). The description takes the form of an extended military metaphor, sustained by the use of phrases like 'hacer la guardia', 'destacarse al aire libre', or 'replegarse con buen ordèn', and culminating in the evocation of 'el terrible campo de batalla, en el cual no hemos de encontrar charcos de sangre ni militares despojos, sino pulgas y otras feroces alimañas' (V, 1878a). The humorous irony is obvious, but it would be wrong to suppose that Galdós's attitude to poverty is a flippant one. The joke is not at the expense of the beggars, but is directed at those who mask the abject and degrading reality of poverty with stereotyped rhetorical images ('el estilo'). If we remain alert to the implications suggested by the tone of the description, we shall be quick to recognize conventional attitudes towards poverty when we encounter them in characters like Don Carlos Moreno Trujillo. Furthermore, we ourselves will avoid sentimentalizing the beggars to the point where we overlook the petty jealousy, enmity and lust for power which characterize many of them.

Galdós, in short, is an exception to the generalization that the nineteenth-century novel demands from the reader no more than a passive kind of receptiveness. If we are to perceive the full range of reference of a Galdós novel, we must read with close attention, not only to factual detail, but above all to the tone and manner of presentation. This notion is reinforced if we consider the second of the techniques I have chosen to discuss, analogy. It is a truism to say that we can only form judgements about particular features of literary works if we consider them in context. What is often overlooked, however, especially in Galdós criticism, is that 'context' embraces more than the immediate texture of irony or metaphor present in particular paragraphs, such as the military imagery described above. The significance of each particular episode, character or relationship must be seen as part of the whole tissue of the work. Now doubtless there are many novels in which a very large proportion of the matter contained between the covers is, to borrow Pooh-Bah's phrase, 'merely corroborative detail, intended to give artistic verisimilitude to an otherwise bald and unconvincing narrative'. Nor is this procedure to be despised: for if the novel purports to represent real life, the social and material fabric of this life must be shown in some detail. With Galdós, however, this corroborative detail is frequently arranged into patterns which set up relationships of analogy between various elements in the novel. The significance of particular pieces of behaviour is thus made to emerge implicitly by juxtaposition with other different but comparable pieces of behaviour.

At the end of *Misericordia*, for example, Benina is supplanted in her role as housekeeper to the ineffectual Doña Paca by the latter's daughter-in-law, Juliana. At one level, Benina and Juliana are alike: both display efficiency and practical common sense, which they put at Doña Paca's disposal in an effort to prevent her succumbing to bewilderment and helplessness, and dissipating her money on fripperies. But the similarity in the actions of the two women only make us more keenly aware that these actions are carried out in a quite different spirit. Benina is loving, kind and self-effacing; Juliana hard, domineering, self-assertive. There are innumerable instances in Galdós's novels where the quality and tone of a particular relationship, such as Benina's ability to confer a spiritual dimension on the most banal everyday tasks, is more effectively conveyed by this kind of analogical juxtaposition than it could be by descriptive or discursive treatment.

Professor Parker has claimed that 'Galdós aimed at bringing not only a wry smile to his reader's lips but also a lump to his throat' (*14*, 22). I would suggest that rather than appealing to the emotions, whether of mockery or sympathy, Galdós is appealing to our judgement. We cannot fall back on a cold intellectual aestheticism, taking pleasure in the skilful weaving of patterns, for Galdós gives us no warrant for thinking that the human issues raised in his novels have nothing to do with us. Equally, however, we are not being invited to rejoice with those who rejoice and weep with those who weep. Galdós, knowing full well that most people would be tempted to respond to novels in this way, took care to induce an alert and circumspect attitude in his reader. The cultivation of an ironic perspective is not meant to make us cynical about human tragedy, but is designed to ensure that our emotions will not interfere with our recognition of the almost limitless complexity of reality, in the presence of which the only mature response is that of silent contemplation: 'la verdad mira y calla'.

CHAPTER II

The World of *M-I-A-U*

... un mundo de una pequeñez
abrumadora (Unamuno).

THE efforts of modern academic critics to settle the question of Villaamil's tragic status would undoubtedly have surprised some of Galdós's contemporaries, not to mention the succeeding generation of writers. Leopoldo Alas, usually a shrewd and perceptive reader of Galdós, failed to see anything of substance in *Miau*, and assumed that Galdós had offered it 'como un entremés, sin esperanza de hacer algo notable'. Alas appears to have found the everyday doings of an impoverished middle-class family lacking in aesthetic appeal or human interest:

> El principal defecto de *Miau* ... consiste en esa especie de delectación morosa con que el autor se detiene a describir y narrar ciertos objetos y acontecimientos que importan poco y no añaden elemento alguno de belleza, ni siquiera de curiosidad a la obra artística. (7, 170-1)

Alas's view would have been endorsed by later writers like Unamuno and Valle-Inclán. It was Valle who coined the notorious quip about 'Don Benito el Garbancero'. [3] Unamuno, for his part, regarded the world of the Galdosian novel as 'un mundo de pequeños tenderos, de pequeños oficinistas, de pequeños usureros o más bien prestamistas; un mundo de una pequeñez abrumadora'. [4]

These criticisms imply that Galdós is at fault for concentrating on trivial everyday matters, instead of the large and important issues commonly treated in serious literature. But Unamuno and Valle-Inclán are mistaken in assuming that Galdós is interested in everyday detail for its own sake. As I have tried to argue in the previous chapter, Galdós's emphasis on the banality of every-

[3] *Luces de Bohemia*, Scene IV.
[4] 'Nuestra impresión de Galdós', *Obras completas*, Vol. V (Madrid, 1952), p. 368.

day existence is part of an ironic scheme for exposing the human capacity for self-deception and self-dramatization, which is anything but a trivial matter. We need to consider the probability of Galdós's having created 'un mundo de una pequeñez abrumadora' as part of a deliberate literary strategy.

The ironic perspective of *Miau* is made clear even by the very title. Theodore A. Sackett has drawn our attention to the fact that Iribarren's *El porqué de los dichos* describes the word *miau* as carrying clear connotations of derision or scepticism (*17, 36*). If Sackett is right in suggesting that Galdós intended to convey these overtones (and his argument is very convincing), then there are grounds for believing that the reader is meant to be on his guard against taking the surface meaning of the novel too literally. Nor is this all. Robert J. Weber (*18,* 12) has suggested that Galdós may have had a particular literary source in mind. In Chapter 18 of *Don Quixote*, Part I, the knight's imagination metamorphoses a flock of sheep into an army, and he names some of the famous warriors who, he believes, are about to give battle on the plain before him. Among them is

> —...Timonel de Carcajona, príncipe de la Nueva Vizcaya, que viene armado con las armas partidas a cuarteles, azules, verdes, blancas, y amarillas, y trae en el escudo un gato de oro en campo leonado, con una letra que dice: *Miau,* que es el principio del nombre de su dama, que, según se dice, es la sin par Miaulina...

This parody of the novels of chivalry is a good example of precisely that Cervantine or deflationary irony which I mentioned earlier. Given that this type of irony is so prevalent in Galdós's novels, given also the frequency of explicitly Cervantine allusions, it seems reasonable to suppose that the choice of title is part of the author's ironic intention.

However that may be, there is little doubt that an ironic perspective is present in the opening pages, and I now want to examine the first chapter in some detail, for it is here that Galdós establishes the main themes that he is going to develop in the course of the novel, and lays down various clues for the reader as to how he is to interpret the material presented to him. Chapter 1 opens with a description of children coming out of

school at the end of the day. Immediately, in the second sentence
of the novel, a mock-heroic note is sounded:

> Ningún himno a la libertad, entre los muchos que se han
> compuesto en las diferentes naciones, es tan hermoso
> como el que entonan los oprimidos de la enseñanza ele-
> mental al soltar el grillete de la disciplina escolar y *echarse
> a la calle* piando y saltando. La furia insana con que se
> lanzan a los más arriesgados ejercicios de volatinería, los
> estropicios que suelen causar a algún pacífico transeúnte,
> el delirio de la autonomía individual que a veces acaba
> en porrazos, lágrimas y cardenales, parecen bosquejo de
> los triunfos revolucionarios que en edad menos dichosa
> han de celebrar los hombres... (65; V, 551a)

This type of language is very similar to the extended military metaphor which I quoted from *Misericordia* in the first
chapter. Furthermore, comparison with the Alpha manuscript
of *Miau* suggests that Galdós deliberately added elements which
would help to sustain the ironic tone (413). The rhetoric of political
revolution is entirely inappropriate to such a commonplace event as
children emerging from school. Notice how the grandiose 'himno
a la libertad... que entonan los oprimidos...' leads into '...de la
enseñanza elemental'. The effect of bathos is cumulative, for
whereas we expect 'soltar el grillete' to be followed by something
like '... de la tiranía', what we actually have is '...de la disciplina
escolar'; and the classic phrase for a revolutionary uprising, 'echar-
se a la calle' is countered by '...piando y saltando'. It would be
pedantic, *pace* Weber (*18*, 82-3), to read this sentence as implying
a comment on education or politics: its sole function is to create
an atmosphere, and a certain set of attitudes and expectations
in the reader, and it does this by the stylistic devices I have
described, even though it is not explicitly linked with the main
events in the novel.

Among the children is the Villaamils' grandson, Luisito Cadalso. When he arrives home, the door is opened by his grand-
mother, Doña Pura. Almost the first thing we are told about
this lady is that her present down-at-heel condition contrasts
markedly with her pretensions of twenty years before:

Veintitantos años antes de lo que aquí se refiere, un periodistín que escribía la cotización de las harinas y las revistas de sociedad, anunciaba de este modo la aparición de aquella dama en los salones del Gobernador de una provincia de tercera clase: '¿Quién es aquella figura arrancada de un cuadro del Beato Angélico, y que viene envuelta en nubes vaporosas y ataviada con el nimbo de oro de la iconografía del siglo xiv?' Las vaporosas nubes eran el vestidillo de gasa que la señora de Villaamil encargó a Madrid por aquellos días, y el áureo nimbo, el demonio me lleve si no era la efusión de la cabellera, que entonces debía de ser rubia y, por tanto, cotizable a la par, literariamente, con el oro de Arabia.

Cuatro o cinco lustros después de estos éxitos de elegancia en aquella ciudad provinciana... doña Pura... llevaba peinador no muy limpio, zapatillas de fieltro no muy nuevas y bata floja de tartán verde. (70; 553a)

Lest we should jump to the conclusion that Doña Pura's present poverty entitles her to our unadulterated sympathy, Galdós carefully structures the description so as to maintain ironic detachment. The humour of 'el demonio me lleve si no era...' is obvious, but one may also point to the slightly contemptuous diminutive 'periodistín', and the fact that Doña Pura's 'éxitos de elegancia' are achieved in a 'provincia de tercera clase'. The fact that the 'revistero de sociedad' also covers the Corn Exchange suggests the insincere and hackneyed nature of his eulogistic descriptions of Doña Pura: he can turn his hand just as easily to one as to the other. Doña Pura's fall from relative affluence to poverty is not, in short, of heroic proportions because the gentility from which she fell is itself tawdry and second-rate.

We may say, indeed, that Galdós is here anticipating the causal connexion, developed in more detail in the main body of the novel, between Doña Pura's decline in prosperity and her petty snobbery and pretentiousness. And this suggestion is confirmed when she greets Luis, immediately after the end of the foregoing quotation, with the words, '¡Ah! Eres tú, Luisín... Yo creí que era Ponce con los billetes del Real'. This utterance not only introduces the figure of Abelarda's insipid fiancé, Ponce,

with all the overtones of *cursilería* which surround that relationship,
but also contains a carefully-placed reference to the opera-going
activities of the three Villaamil women. These frequent visits to
the gods of the Teatro Real serve a dual function in the novel.
They remind us of the constant social posturing of *Las Miaus*,
even in the midst of their near-destitution, for the three women
go to the opera to be seen by their acquaintances, and to maintain in public a façade of normality and respectability, an effort
which is quite nugatory, of course, because the public is not
taken in. Secondly, opera represents an ideal romantic world
into which the women, especially Milagros and Abelarda, can
immerse themselves in order to escape from the practical realities of existence. When Doña Pura resolves one particularly
severe crisis by borrowing from Carolina Pez,

> ...Abelarda y Milagros... se tranquilizaron respecto al pro-
> blema de subsistencias de aquel día, y se pusieron a cantar,
> la una en la cocina, la otra desde su cuarto, el dúo de
> *Norma: in mia mano al fin tu sei.* (115; 569b)

Well may Villaamil later say, 'Éstas, con su música y sus tonte-
rías, no sirven para nada' (387; 673b-4a).

The unheroic atmosphere is so deliberately built up in this
opening chapter that we are not surprised to find that the presentation of Don Ramón is also affected by it. The first indication
of his presence is 'una voz cavernosa y sepulcral' which emerges
from the darkened study where he is writing begging letters to
various people who he hopes will help him to get his job back.
In the fading light, his figure stands out as 'un sombrajo largui-
rucho'. The comic and grotesque overtones of the suffixes *-ajo*
and *-ucho* are reinforced when we find that this 'temerosa y
empañada voz' begins with rather petulant, mundane complaints
that Doña Pura has not thought of bringing him a lamp. We
then move into a more detailed physical description, the keynote
of which is the contrast between the fierce outward appearance
and the real ineffectualness of the man:

> La robustez de la mandíbula, el grandor de la boca, la
> combinación de los tres colores: negro, blanco y amarillo,

dispuestos en rayas, la ferocidad de los ojos negros, indu-
cían a comparar tal cara con la de un tigre viejo y tísico
que, después de haberse lucido en las exhibiciones ambu-
lantes de fieras, no conserva ya de su antigua belleza más
que la pintorreada piel. (73; 554b)

A little later, an even more explicitly mock-heroic note is struck:

El tigre inválido se transfiguraba. Tenía la expresión subli-
me de un apóstol en el momento en que le están martiri-
zando por la fe, algo del San Bartolomé de Ribera cuando
le suspenden del árbol y le descueran aquellos tunantes
de gentiles, como si fuera un cabrito. (75; 555a)

This is as typical an example as one is likely to find of Galdós's habit of comparing the demeanour of a character with a
particular artistic representation. It is not that Villaamil is consciously modelling himself on the Ribera painting; in that case
he would be an insincere poseur. What the comparison does
achieve, however, is to remind us of how easily the expression
of emotion, even genuine emotion, conforms to conventional
stereotypes. We might uncritically take Villaamil's part if we
felt that his exteriorization of his feelings was free of cliché; as
it stands, the comic distancing effected in this passage makes
us feel that 'it's been done before'. Moreover, even if Villaamil
is not deliberately striking a pose, there is a sense in which he
is prone to self-dramatization. It is significant that most of the
references to the injustice of his dismissal come from Villaamil
himself. The organization of the novel encourages us to perceive
Villaamil, not as a victim of arbitrariness and ingratitude, but
as a person who sees himself as such a victim. Immediately prior
to the Ribera passage, he bangs the table, and exclaims: 'En este
mundo no hay más que egoísmo, ingratitud, y mientras más
infamias se ven, más quedan por ver' (74; 555a), unconsciously
anticipating almost identical words used in the very next chapter
by the ape-like reactionary Mendizábal, 'que solía repetir las
frases del periódico a que estaba suscrito' (79; 556a). [5]

[5] The parallel between Villaamil's words and Mendizábal's appears to have
been added in the Beta manuscript, though it is impossible to be certain, since
some leaves are missing from Alpha at this point (420-1).

So much for the first chapter. As we move through the novel, we find that the anti-heroic perspective established at the beginning is carefully sustained. Thus immediately after Don Ramón has told us, in one of his frequent soliloquies, that he needs only two months' active service to be able to retire on four-fifths of his salary, we have a reference to 'una cómoda jubilada con los cuatro quintos de su cajonería' (97; 563a). Like Doña Pura, her sister Milagros is presented in terms of a contrast between her present position and her previous expectations. The provincial *periodistín* whom we encountered earlier, when he is not writing about prices on the Corn Exchange, finds time to christen Milagros 'la pudorosa Ofelia' (113; 568a). Luis's napkin is tied not round his 'cuello', but around his 'pescuezo' (114; 569a), a word normally only used of animals. The Villaamils' commonplace acquaintances are referred to as 'la escogida sociedad que frecuentaba... aquella elegante mansión' (252; 621b). The death of the soprano in *L'Africaine* is expressed by the verb *espichar*, which is extremely colloquial, even for Galdós (278; 632b). Guillén's deliberate mistake in claiming that Don Ramón was born in Coria rather than Burgos is described as a 'garrafal dislate histórico' (333; 653a).

Perhaps the most characteristic of these pieces of parody is the description of Don Ramón walking along the corridors of the Ministry building with his friend Argüelles, whom Galdós earlier called 'perfecta parodia de un caballero del tiempo de Felipe IV' (226-7; 611b), because he affects the tonsorial style of that period:

> A lo largo del pasadizo accidentado y misterioso, las figu-ras de Villaamil y de Argüelles habrían podido trocarse, por obra y gracia de hábil caricatura, en las de Dante y Virgilio buscando por senos recónditos la entrada o salida de los recintos infernales que visitaban. No era difícil hacer de don Ramón un burlesco Dante por lo escueto de la figura y por la amplia capa que le envolvía; pero, en lo tocante al poeta, había que substituirle con Quevedo, pa-rodiador de la *Divina Comedia*, si bien el bueno de Argüelles más semejanza tenía con el *Alguacil alguacilado* que con el gran vate que lo inventó. Ni Dante ni Quevedo soñaron,

en sus fantásticos viajes, nada parecido al laberinto ofici-
nesco, al campaneo discorde de los timbres... y al tráfago
y zumbido, en fin, de estas colmenas donde se labra el
panal amargo de la Administración. (341; 655b-6a)

The parody in this passage operates in several complex ways.
The world of government offices is devalued by the burlesque
evocation of the *Divine Comedy*, but this devaluation is carried
two stages further, for Argüelles is really like not Virgil, but
Quevedo, 'parodiador de la *Divina Comedia*'; he is a parody of a
parodist. Then, with the conjunction 'si bien', Galdós shifts the
focus again: Argüelles is not even fit to be compared to 'el gran
vate', but is more like one of his satirical creations. Finally, in
the last sentence of the quotation, another and more disquieting
twist is given to the presentation. If the world of administration
seems vulgar and commonplace beside the apocalyptic visions
of the *Divine Comedy*, it possesses its own particular kind of
mundane horror, undreamt of by Dante or Quevedo. In the
particular context which Galdós has established, the otherwise
hackneyed metaphors of the labyrinth and the beehive acquire
their full literal force, and express something starkly real. The
office building comes to seem a trap from which the workers
cannot escape, and the only fruit of their mindless and feverish
activity is a useless 'panal amargo'.

This use of imagery reveals the true significance of the ironic
dimension in *Miau*, and provides an answer to those critics who
insist that we must choose between a comic and a tragic reading
of the novel. The evocation of Quevedo is particularly apposite,
for it reminds us that satire, at its best, transcends clever joke-
making, and expresses a deep concern with the moral health of
mankind. While Galdós would not have gone as far as some
of his contemporaries in using the novel for explicitly didactic
purposes, he retained to the end of his life a conviction that
serious literature had an important educational function. 'La lite-
ratura', he declared in 1912, 'debe ser enseñanza, ejemplo'. [6]
This moral purpose, he believed, is best achieved by a judicious

[6] Luis Antón del Olmet and Arturo García Carraffa, *Galdós* (Madrid, 1912),
p. 93.

mixture of the comic and the serious. By contrast with the solemn lubricity of French naturalism,

> nuestro arte de la naturalidad, con su feliz concierto entre lo serio y lo cómico, responde mejor que el francés a la verdad humana; que las crudezas descriptivas pierden toda repugnancia bajo la máscara burlesca empleada por Quevedo, y que los profundos estudios psicológicos pueden llegar a la mayor perfección con los granos de sal española que escritores como don Juan Valera saben poner hasta en las más hondas disertaciones sobre cosa mística y ascética. (*6*, 216; VI, 1460b)

We have, of course, no warrant for supposing that Galdós deliberately modelled himself on Quevedo, and the cultural climate in which each writer worked is obviously very different. But the comparison is nevertheless useful. Like Quevedo, Galdós employs deflationary irony in the service of an overall moral vision. More specifically, Galdós is concerned that we should not become so involved in the fortunes of any one character as to be distracted from the main purpose of the novel, which is to reveal an entire society engaged in the self-indulgent pursuit of trivial and unworthy values. The extended parody I quoted earlier is made possible only by the fact that Argüelles (a key character who has received remarkably little attention from critics) is so vain that he deliberately makes himself up to look like a seventeenth-century gentleman. The Dantean or Quevedesque associations of the passage thus lead us back to the whole theme of social posturing exemplified elsewhere in the novel by the opera-going of the *Miaus* and the second-hand elegance of Víctor.

Irony and analogy are thus in the last analysis not two separate techniques, but two prongs of the same instrument, so to speak. The ironic detachment enables us to stand far enough back from the characters to see the broad similarities between them, and to realize that, taken together, they add up to a particular kind of society. Even more significantly, however, viewing the total picture from a certain distance makes us aware of the shades and gradations along the spectrum of *presunción*, and of the ease with which relatively innocuous forms of vanity can lead, by a series of small steps, to more serious and destructive ones. If Argüelles's vanity is harmless enough, that of Víctor Cadalso is calamitous in its consequences. This plausible southerner would hardly have seemed so handsome and distinguished had he had to compete for attention in any sphere other than 'una capital de provincia de tercera clase, ciudad arqueológica, de corto y no muy brillante vecindario' (166; 588b). As it is, his superficial attractions completely captivate the ignorant and gullible Luisa Villaamil, resulting in a passionate love-affair, a hasty wedding, and an unhappy marriage which ends in Luisa's insanity and death.

The connexions between the various blocks of experience which make up the novel are so skilfully established and so carefully controlled that a rigid dichotomy between comedy and tragedy is entirely inapplicable to *Miau*. We cannot, for example, re-read the passage from Chapter 1 in which Villaamil is caricatured as a 'tigre viejo y tísico' without realizing that he was reduced to this condition by Luisa's death, brought on by Víctor's neglect and infidelity:

> sin ruidoso duelo exterior, mudo y con los ojos casi secos, se desquició y desplomó interiormente, quedándose como ruina lamentable, sin esperanza, sin ilusión ninguna de la vida; y desde entonces se le secó el cuerpo hasta momificarse, y fue tomando su cara aquel aspecto de ferocidad famélica que le asemejaba a un tigre anciano e inútil. (171; 590b)

This tight organic structure means that it is more than usually perverse of the critic to deal with characters or issues separately, but it is difficult to see what practicable alternative there is. Since Villaamil is the centre round which the other elements in the novel are grouped, it seems appropriate at this juncture to proceed to a more detailed analysis of his role.

CHAPTER III

Villaamil

Por fuerza tiene que haber un
enemigo oculto (*Miau*, Chapter 4).

Don Ramón is undoubtedly the most central character in the
novel, but it does not follow that the most important issue
raised in *Miau* is the justice or injustice of his dismissal from
the public service, as many critics seem to assume. Ramsden, for
example, argues that since there is nothing in the novel to indi-
cate that Villaamil's dismissal was on grounds of incompetence, a
clear injustice exists (15, 66). This statement is certainly hard
to refute, but it makes insufficient allowance for the nature of
literary evidence. As readers of novels, we do not have the
freedom to establish the evidence for a particular interpretation
by bringing new and relevant facts to light, as we might do in
real life. The evidence has been deliberately selected and arranged by the novelist so as to manipulate us into perceiving
things from a certain angle. If the reasons for Villaamil's dismissal
are deliberately left vague, it is because Galdós does not wish
us to speculate on them, but to pay attention to other issues.

I have already suggested in the previous chapter what these
issues might be. Villaamil is presented above all as a person who
sees himself as the victim of injustice, and it is this, rather than
injustice in any objective sense, that provides the main focus of
interest. It is significant in this regard that most of our informa-
tion on Villaamil's career, and on his feelings about his dismissal,
comes from Don Ramón himself. From the third-person narrative we learn that he has been comparatively lucky throughout
his career in having been unemployed only for short periods,
at least until the present; and that his efforts to support his
family in decent comfort have been negated by his wife's extravagance. On the other hand, virtually all references to his honesty
and conscientiousness not only come from his own lips, but

occur in the midst of long monologues in which he complains bitterly about his treatment. He is hardly an unbiassed witness, and it is thus difficult for the reader to separate any feelings he may have about the arbitrariness of Villaamil's dismissal from the clear impression of Don Ramón's self-pity and self-drama-tization, conveyed through the selective presentation.

Villaamil's reaction to his dismissal is, moreover, clearly seen to be a function of his pessimistic temperament, and this is cor-roborated when we compare him with the other perennial *cesan-te* in the novel, Federico Ruiz. Ruiz is clearly to some extent a figure of fun, and when his subsequent re-employment coin-cides with his achieving the preposterous title of *Bombeiro, salva-dor da humanidade*, simply by virtue of having written a monograph on fire-fighting, we are meant to infer a satirical comment on the general fatuousness of society at large. We are not, however, thereby precluded from discerning other elements in Ruiz's role. His happy-go-lucky attitude to his unemployment reminds us that Villaamil's jeremiads are not the only possible response to the situation. There is, of course, no question of attributing praise to one and blame to the other. Villaamil's circumstances are very different: his wife, unlike Pepita Ruiz, is far from being a model of economy and efficiency. Conversely, there is some-thing conventional and self-deceiving about Ruiz's assumption that virtuous poverty is to be preferred, which is simply another commonplace of second-rate romantic literature. The fact remains that the effect of the juxtaposition between these two reactions to unemployment is to make Don Ramón appear obsessional about public service in a way that Federico is not. Both haunt government offices in the hope of re-employment, but Ruiz also develops other interests: indeed, one may say that it is precisely because of the fatuity of society that such varied op-portunities are available to anyone prepared to adopt Ruiz's easy-going approach.

Don Ramón lacks Ruiz's panache and journalistic facility, and while the absence of these qualities is to some extent at-tributable to his circumstances and training, the main emphasis falls on his temperamental incapacity for functioning outside the world of the government office. Critics often draw attention to the fact that Villaamil fails to put a stop to Pura's extravagance, or to assert mastery of his own house in the face of Víctor's intrusion. Rather than use this as evidence for Villaamil's suitability or unsuitability for re-employment, however, an issue on which, as I have suggested, there are scant grounds for a clear judgement, I would prefer to say that it illustrates the discontinuity between Villaamil's professional and non-professional selves. Reality is perceived by him exclusively from the standpoint of his *cesantía*, and he cannot come to terms with relationships or areas of experience which lie outside this concern. Even his begging letters are couched in civil service jargon, and when, just before his suicide, he evokes the figure of his grandson Luis, his imaginary speech to the boy is partly cast in epistolary moulds: '... y ya sabes dónde me tienes... Siempre tuyo...' (410; 682b)

Now it is very tempting to confine one's discussion of the obsessional nature of Villaamil's desire for re-employment to that part of the novel where this obsession is most obvious: the last quarter of the text, beginning with Villaamil's outburst of rage in Pantoja's office at the end of Chapter 34, shows him gradually losing his mental balance until he finally takes his own life. It is easy enough to argue that it is the inhumanity of the State that has reduced him to this pass. What is often overlooked, however, is that from the very outset, Villaamil has shown a tendency to be so wrapped up in his preoccupation with regaining what he regards as his rightful position in the State hierarchy that he is indifferent to other people.

One of the clearest examples of this occurs in Chapter 4, where he is left to put Luis to bed after the women have gone to the opera. As he undresses the boy, he broods aloud on his misfortunes:

> —Hijo mío, ve aprendiendo, ve aprendiendo para cuando seas hombre. Del que está caído nadie se acuerda, y lo que hacen es patearle y destrozarle para que no se pueda levantar... Figúrate tú que yo debiera ser jefe de Administración de segunda, pues ahora me tocaría ascender con arreglo a la ley de Cánovas del 76, y aquí me tienes pereciendo... ¡Yo, que el 55 hice un plan de presupuestos que mereció los elogios del señor don Pascual Madoz y

del señor don Juan Bruil, plan que en veinte años de me-
ditaciones he rehecho después, explanándolo en cuatro
memorias que ahí tengo! Y no es cosa de broma. Supre-
sión de todas las contribuciones actuales, substituyéndolas
con el *income tax*... Luego, la renta de Aduanas, bien refor-
zada, con los derechos muy altos para proteger la indus-
tria nacional... Y por último, la unificación de las Deudas,
reduciéndolas a un tipo de emisión y a un tipo de interés...

Al llegar aquí tiró Villaamil con tanta fuerza de los
pantalones de Luis, que el niño lanzó un ¡ay! diciendo:

—Abuelo, que me arrancas las piernas.

A lo que el irritado viejo contestó secamente:

—Por fuerza tiene que haber un enemigo oculto, algún
trasto que se ha propuesto hundirme, deshonrarme... (98-9;
563b-4a)

This passage should not be considered in isolation, as it is
really the culmination of several hours of brooding which begins
at the end of Chapter 1, when immediate economic necessity
forces Villaamil to ask for a loan from Cucúrbitas. It is very
noticeable that Villaamil's mind constantly strays away from
specifically economic matters into the sphere of administrative
grades and promotion, dwelling especially on the careers of
former subordinates, usually incompetent, who have overtaken
him in the ascent of the civil service ladder. Notice how economic matters are intermingled with considerations of Villaamil's
status in relation to former colleagues in the following lament
to Doña Pura in Chapter 1:

—Ya ves la que me hizo ayer ese badulaque de Rubín.
Le pinto nuestra necesidad; pongo mi cara en vergüenza
suplicándole..., nada, un pequeño anticipo, y... Sabe Dios
la hiel que uno traga antes de decidirse..., y lo que padece
la dignidad... Pues ese ingrato, ese olvidadizo, a quien
tuve de escribiente en mi oficina siendo yo Jefe de nego-
ciado de cuarta, ese desvergonzado que por su audacia ha
pasado por delante de mí, llegando nada menos que a
Gobernador, tiene la poca delicadeza de mandarme medio
duro. (74; 554b)

His next speech takes him even further away from the immediate economic problem, to which he has to recall himself by
a conscious effort:

> —En este mundo no hay más que egoísmo, ingratitud,
> y mientras más infamias se ven, más quedan por ver...
> Como ese bigardón de Montes, que me debe su carrera,
> pues yo le propuse para el ascenso en la Contaduría Cen-
> tral. ¿Creerás tú que ya ni siquiera me saluda? Se da una
> importancia, que ni el Ministro... Y va siempre adelante.
> Acaban de darle catorce mil. Cada año su ascensito, y ole
> morena... Éste es el premio de la adulación y la bajeza.
> No sabe palotada de administración; no sabe más que
> hablar de caza con el Director, y de la galga y del pájaro
> y qué sé yo qué... Tiene peor ortografía que un perro, y
> escribe *hacha* sin *h* y *echar* con ella... Pero, en fin, dejemos
> a un lado estas miserias. (74-5; 555a)

That economic considerations are secondary for Don Ramón is
borne out when on the following day his wife, having borrowed
money from Carolina Pez, presents him with an opulent lunch.
Where the money came from, why it has been spent on 'abun-
dancias tan disconformes con su situación económica' (118; 570a),
and how it is to be repaid, are matters which ought to concern
Villaamil as head of the household. But it does not occur to him
even to wonder, much less to ask, about this unusual affluence.

This indifference to anything other than his reintegration
into the hierarchy of the public service is the keynote of the
scene with Luis in Chapter 4, from which I quoted above.
Villaamil is barely conscious of the child's presence, pulling off
Luis's clothes so violently that he hurts him. Nor is he aware of
the absurdity of bombarding his uncomprehending grandson with
the technical jargon of government finance. And the reference
to 'un enemigo oculto' is the first of many examples of Villaamil's
persecution complex, which grows in intensity as the novel
proceeds.

Another aspect of Villaamil's obsession which emerges at a
similarly early stage is his superstitious habit of trying deliberately to think himself into a pessimistic view of things, so that,
as he believes, he may have a better chance of being surprised

by good news. The first instance of this occurs in Chapter 4, just after Luis has gone to sleep. Villaamil has to struggle hard to maintain this pose, for his irresistible desire to regain his job keeps breaking through, leading to an even more energetic assertion of his studied pessimism. The following dialogue takes place on the evening after the scene with Luis:

—¿Qué hay? ¿Qué noticias traes?

—Nada, mujer —dijo Villaamil, que se encastillaba en el pesimismo y no había quien le sacara de él—. Todavía nada; las palabritas sandungueras de siempre.

—¿Y el Ministro...? ¿Le has visto?

—Sí, y me recibió tan bien —se dejó decir Villaamil haciendo traición, por descuido, a su afectada misantropía—, me recibió tan bien que... no sé..., parece que Dios le ha tocado al corazón...

—Vamos; no dirás ahora que no tienes esperanza.

—Ninguna, mujer, absolutamente ninguna (recobrando su papel). (125; 572b)

Taken out of context, this scene is comic, but Villaamil's studied pessimism comes to seem much more self-destructive when it interferes with his attempts to take decisive action when this is called for. The reason why Víctor is able to gain the upper hand over his father-in-law in their first dispute is that he can skilfully play on this quirk of Villaamil's, and thus turn the debate away from the issue of his own fraudulent activities:

—Te repito de una vez para siempre... que yo no espero nada, ni pienso que me colocarán jamás. En cambio estoy convencido de que tú, tú, que acabas de defraudar al Tesoro, tendrás el premio de tu gracia, porque así es el mundo, y así está la cochina Administración... Adiós (marchándose y volviendo desde la puerta). Y ten entendido que yo no espero ni esto; que estoy conforme, que llevo con paciencia mi desgracia, y que no se me ocurre que me puedan colocar ahora, ni mañana, ni el siglo que viene..., aunque buena falta nos hace. (150-1; 583a)

So sedulously does Villaamil cultivate this pessimistic pose that it eventually rebounds upon him. He comes to believe that he will never regain his post, and that a corrupt Administration is bent on humiliating and destroying him. His pessimism thus comes to appear as an aspect of his persecution complex, each element reinforcing the other. This is the real significance of the four memoranda on fiscal reform which Villaamil has written, and to which he constantly refers throughout the novel. Despite the laborious attempts by critics to prove that Don Ramón's ideas are either sensible or naive in relation to the actual state of Spanish finance in the 1870s, I remain unconvinced that Galdós was primarily concerned with Villaamil's acumen in fiscal matters, since he tells us virtually nothing about the practical value of these memoranda. As always, we must take account of the context in which the issue is presented. The first mention of Villaamil's proposal for the introduction of Income Tax occurs in that very scene with Luis which I mentioned earlier, where, as we saw, the main emphasis falls on the obsessional and self-centred nature of Don Ramón's preoccupation with the administration of the country. [7]

A more extended treatment is given in Chapter 22. Villaamil, unable to be away for long from the only sphere in which he feels at home, has taken to haunting the Ministry building, picking up bits of gossip and news, most of which tend to confirm his bleak view of things. His solemn and rather rhetorical approach to his own problems quickly makes him the butt of merciless teasing on the part of the office staff, a fact which he characteristically does not realize, because of his self-preoccupation. The teasing tends to centre on the memoranda, because the employees know that Villaamil can be relied upon to entertain them with a pompous summary of their contents. Their mock praise on this occasion draws from Don Ramón the following somewhat fatuous speech:

> —No es que sepa mucho (con modestia); es que miro las cosas *de la casa* como mías propias, y quisiera ver a este país entrar de lleno por la senda del orden. Esto no es ciencia, es buen deseo, aplicación, trabajo. Ahora bien: ¿ustedes me hicieron caso? Pues ellos tampoco. Allá se

---

[7] There is no mention of Income Tax in Alpha (433).

las hayan. Llegará día en que los españoles tengan que
andar descalzos y los más ricos pedir para ayuda de un
panecillo...; digo, no pedirán limosna, porque no habrá
quien la dé. (241; 617b)

High-minded and well-meaning this certainly is, but Don
Ramón is deluding himself if he imagines that a modest *Jefe de
Administración de tercera* has the power to save the country from
bankruptcy, however many memoranda he writes. The last half
of the passage, with its implied washing of hands ('allá se las
hayan') and prognostications of future calamity, is couched in
the familiar language of paranoia. His future 'madness', in short,
is simply the intensification of a tendency which is well established at a much earlier stage. Well before his final breakdown,
he is capable of using language which is just as violent as anything
he says in the last hours of his life. When, for example, one of
Pantoja's subordinates leads him on by hinting at the possibility
of a major political upheaval, Villaamil exclaims:

—Así saltara esta noche el cantón de Madrid y la
Commune inclusive, y tocaran a pegar fuego... Les digo a
ustedes que el amigo Job era un niño mimado y se queja-
ba de vicio... Que venga el santo petróleo, que venga.
(269; 629a)

It has been argued with some conviction that Don Ramón's
suicide is a liberation from the vicious circle of enslavement to
the State (*3*, 273-4; *14*, 16). This, however, is to take him at
his own evaluation. Despite his claims that he has regained his
freedom, it is clear that the State is still at the centre of his
thoughts. His decision to kill himself is apparently taken on the
day following his outburst in Pantoja's office, for it is then that
he buys the revolver. By now, he has begun to affect a lofty
detachment from his previous sufferings, but this is not the serene
detachment which comes from the ending of a struggle. The paranoia which Villaamil displayed earlier is now greatly intensified.
He declares to Argüelles and Sevillano:

—Yo lo acepto. Esa M, esa I, esa A y esa U son,
como el *Inri*, el letrero infamante que le pusieron a Cristo

> en la cruz... Ya que me han crucificado entre ladrones,
> para que todo sea completo, pónganme sobre la cabeza
> esas cuatro letras en que se hace mofa y escarnio de mi
> gran misión. (344; 657a)

Moreover, this studied serenity easily breaks down. When he
is told that Víctor owes his promotion to a grotesque affair with
an old lady of over sixty, he says,

> —Si yo me sorprendiera de esto... sería un niño de
> teta. ¡Y esa fantasma ha venido aquí, al templo de la
> Administración (indignándose), a arrojar sobre el Estado la
> ignominia de sus recomendaciones en favor de un perdis!
> (348; 658b)

The clearest indication, however, that Villaamil has not achieved
any real liberation of spirit is that he intends his suicide to appear as a gesture towards the State. Even though this gesture is
one of rejection and contempt, the fact that he feels the need
to make it at all suggests that his frame of reference is fundamentally the same as it has always been:

> —... yo quiero que vea el mundo una cosa, y es que
> ya me importa un pepino que se nivelen o no los presu-
> puestos, y que me río del *income tax* y de toda la indecente
> Administración. (402; 679b)

Now it is a remarkable fact that all the critics who mention
Villaamil's insanity and suicide take it as confirming their interpretation of the novel, whether they regard him as a martyr or
a fool. The *villaamilistas*, if one may so describe them, while
admitting that he is petulant and tiresome, argue that he is made
that way by circumstances, and is consequently all the more
tragic. For the *anti-villaamilistas*, Don Ramón's loss of rational
control is proof that he is irresponsible and incapable of orga-
nizing his life in a mature and effective way. If the argument
of the previous chapter is valid, however, we shall need to
leave room for both perspectives in our thinking about Villaamil.
The ironic tone of the novel makes it clear that Don Ramón
is not the stuff of which traditional tragic heroes are made. On

the other hand, we cannot ascribe his death solely to his personal limitations and mistakes. Obsessional and self-preoccupied he may be, but he is imprisoned in his situation not only by his temperament, but also by the expectations and attitudes of the social class to which he belongs. Federico Ruiz's resilience may protect him against the despair which destroys Villaamil, but the fact remains that both men are at one in making re-employment in the public service the main goal in their lives. If Villaamil's story has some of the depth and seriousness of tragedy, it is not because he is unjustly excluded from a post he deserves to have, but because he is so totally absorbed in the pursuit of his goal that he cannot see that it is unworthy of such single-minded dedication, particularly since it is also the goal of many of his 'normal' contemporaries.

Here again, the pattern of analogy in the novel is illuminating. Somewhere along the line of gradation which links Villaamil with Federico Ruiz comes Argüelles, whose bitter denunciations of *polacadas* in the Administration differ little from Villaamil's. Here, for example, is how Argüelles greets the news of a particularly egregious promotion:

> —Le tuve yo en mi oficina con cinco mil hace catorce años— dijo el *padre de familia*, esgrimiendo su puño cerrado y revelando toda la aflicción del mundo en su cara alguacilesca—. Era tan asno, que le ocupábamos en traer leña para la estufa. Ni para eso servía. ¡Cáscaras, qué hombre más animal! Yo cobraba entonces doce mil, lo mismo que ahora. Vean ustedes si esto es justicia o qué. ¿Tengo o no tengo razón cuando digo que vale más recoger boñiga en las calles que servir al gran pindongo del Estado? (228; 612a-b)

That Argüelles, who at least has a job, can talk like this makes it easier to understand why the unemployed Villaamil should express his views with such vehemence. But Argüelles has also another function. It is he who expresses most clearly the notion that public service is the only means of social acceptance open to those who, while lacking wealth, rank or influence, are nevertheless led by their education to seek to improve their position in the social scale. Immediately after the above speech, he goes on, '¡Cuando me acuerdo, ¡cascarones!, de que mi padre quería colocarme de hortera en una tienda, y yo me remonté creyendo que esto no era cosa fina!' The indignation felt by Argüelles and Villaamil at the spectacle of being overtaken in the race for promotion by incompetent subordinates does not stem entirely from concern with the moral health of the State, but is in part due to a sense of personal betrayal. At first glance, the civil service seems to offer opportunities for gifted men of modest background to acquire status as a reward for their ability, but in practice promotion is achieved by corrupt influences. Villaamil's frustration occasionally takes the form of regret that, having proceeded on one set of assumptions, he does not know how to work the quite different rules which actually operate:

> ... en medio de su catoniana indignación, pensando en aquella ignominia de las faldas corruptoras, se preguntaba por qué no habría también faldas benéficas que, favore- ciendo a los buenos, como él, sirvieran a la Administración y al país. (269; 628b)

It is at first sight very remarkable that in a novel in which the civil service bulks so large, we are told very little about how the country is actually administered. But as A. F. Lambert has pointed out, one of the constants of the anti-bureaucratic tradition to which *Miau*, in part, belongs, is that the civil service is presented, not as a device for running the country, but as a mechanism for giving people jobs (*13*, 44). It is, in modern economic parlance, overmanned, if people like Guillén have time to compose satirical verses or 'algún dramón espeluznante' (226; 611b). However, Galdós, as always, goes further than the liter- ary tradition. When Argüelles says 'me metí a empleado por aquello de ser caballero', he is reflecting a preoccupation with respectability which is not confined to the civil service, but runs through social relationships of all kinds. Abelarda resigns herself to marrying the colourless Ponce 'por colocarse, por tener posi- ción y nombre, y salir de aquella estrechez insoportable de su hogar' (205-6; 603b-4a). In striving to maintain the furnishings of her drawing-room intact, Doña Pura is seeking to *colocarse*, in the sense of expressing her exact relationship with those closest to her in the social hierarchy. When the *Miaus* take their seats in the gods of the Teatro Real, they are *colocándose* in more than a physical sense.

Argüelles's role as a focus for the theme of social status tells us a great deal about how Galdós wants us to view Villaamil. The fact that Don Ramón does *not* consciously subscribe to such ideas suggests that he is unaware of the extent to which he is caught up in large-scale social and cultural pressures. This has the effect of strengthening the tragic element in his portrayal. This tragic aspect is complemented by the comic detachment in two ways. Firstly, we are encouraged not to concentrate excessively on Villaamil as an individual, but to see him as part of a large-scale social and moral problem.[8] Secondly, the way in which Villaamil's high-minded conception of the Administration is constantly punctured by the author's irony ensures that our attention will be directed away from the issue of unemployment to that of mis-employment. To the extent that Don Ramón is tragic, his tragedy is not that of unmerited suffering, but of a wasted life. In attaching a value to phrases like *la casa, el probo y sufrido personal de Hacienda* or *el templo de la Administración*, he has displayed a weakness for constructing his view of reality out of clichés which are clearly seen to have no basis in fact.

In this respect, too, Don Ramón is a representative figure, for the fortunes of certain other characters, principally Abelarda and Víctor, suggest that attachment to cliché is the governing principle of human relationships. This will be considered in the next chapter.

---

[8] Lambert speaks of 'the tension between detached contempt for the bureaucrat and sympathetic identification with him as in many ways a representative modern man', as something which Galdós may well have inherited from Mesonero's contributions to the anti-bureaucratic tradition (*13*, 39).

CHAPTER IV

Abelarda and Víctor

... jugar con los sentimientos
serios y profundos (*Miau,*
Chapter 20).

THE opera-going of the three *Miaus* not only expresses an
attempt to define their social status, but is in part an escape
from the drudgery of their home-life. Doña Pura is described
as one of those people

> ... que atesoran en sí mismas un arsenal de armas espiri-
> tuales contra las penas de la vida y poseen el arte de trans-
> formar los hechos, reduciéndolos y asimilándolos en virtud
> de la facultad dulcificante que en sus entrañas llevan, como
> la abeja, que cuanto chupa lo convierte en miel. (284;
> 634b)

While nothing as explicit as this is said about Milagros and Abelarda, the capacity for escaping mentally from their immediate
surroundings and problems is shared by all three women: we
have already seen how Abelarda and Milagros launch into a
duet from *Norma* as soon as one particularly severe economic
crisis recedes.

When we first meet Abelarda, she seems, outwardly at least,
to be resigned to her drab existence, but Víctor's arrival acts
as a catalyst which stimulates visions of an alternative life, infi-
nitely more interesting and glamorous than anything she has
experienced. This has the effect of making her even more conscious of the vulgarity of her home-life:

> Siempre que Víctor entraba en la casa mirábale Abelarda
> cual si llegase de regiones sociales muy superiores. En su
> andar, lo mismo que en sus modales; en su ropa, lo mismo
> que en su cabellera, traía Víctor algo que se despegaba
> de la pobre vivienda de las *Miaus*, algo que reñía con
> aquel hogar destartalado y pedestre. (185; 595b)

Víctor's air of distinction is, of course, a hollow façade. As I have already suggested, he is fickle, plausible and self-seeking, qualities which have already had disastrous consequences for the Villaamil family in the loss of Luisa. In one respect, however, there is an analogy between Víctor and Abelarda, for he too is something of a dreamer:

> ...toda la vida se la llevaba pensando en riquezas que no tenía, en honores y poder que deseaba, en mujeres hermosas, cuyas seducciones no le eran desconocidas, en damas elegantes y de alta alcurnia que con ardentísima curiosidad anhelaba tratar y poseer, y esta aspiración a los supremos goces de la vida le traía siempre intranquilo, vigilante y en acecho. Devorado por el ansia de introducirse en las clases superiores de la sociedad, creía tener ya en las manos un cabo y el primer nudo de la cuerda por donde otros menos audaces habían logrado subir. (154-5; 584b-5a)

This *cuerda* is Víctor's absurd liaison with a libidinous old dame of over sixty, to whom he owes the covering-up of his embezzlement of State funds in Valencia, and his re-instatement in the civil service at a higher rank than his previous one. This is, at one level, Galdós's most damning comment on the corruption which allows characters like Víctor to flourish, but it should not be overlooked that in common with Abelarda, Villaamil, and virtually all the other characters in the novel, Víctor forms part of a general pattern of aspiration for improvement in life-style, however strongly his cynicism may contrast with their naivety. As we have seen, Abelarda resigns herself to marriage with Ponce because it offers a prospect of escape from the humdrum surroundings of her home.

By establishing this analogy between the various characters, Galdós has made it possible for the reader to avoid dismissing Abelarda's imaginative life as the vapid day-dreams of a silly girl. [9] Indeed, he goes to some lengths to emphasize the idea that

---

[9] Gerald Gillespie's claim that Abelarda's 'distorsionada imagen de la vida, sus hábitos cursis y sus reacciones maniáticas la convierten en una criatura despreciable' is a classic example of the tendency of academic critics to pay insufficient attention to presentation, tone and context. ('*Miau:* hacia una definición de la sensibilidad de Galdós', *Cuadernos Hispanoamericanos*, 250-2 (1970-1), pp. 415-29 (p. 426).)

this interior life has its own reality. When rehearsing for the domestic play-performance which the Villaamils are planning, Abelarda

> asistía a los ensayos como un autómata, prestándose dócil-
> mente a la vida de aquel mundo para ella secundario y arti-
> ficial; como si su casa, su familia, su tertulia, Ponce, fuesen la
> verdadera comedia, de fáciles y rutinarios papeles... y per-
> maneciese libre el espíritu, empapado en su vida interior,
> verdadera y real, en el drama exclusivamente suyo, palpi-
> tante de interés, que no tenía más que un actor: ella; y
> un solo espectador: Dios. (201; 601b-2a)

For all her *cursilería*, the portrayal of Abelarda is one of Galdós's most delicate and complex pieces of characterization. *La
insignificante* comes close to acquiring tragic status, for while her
lack of education and experience precludes her seeing through
Víctor's pose, she retains enough insight to realize that she is
imprisoned in her circle of mediocrity:

> Sí, por más que él diga que no, vulgo soy, y ¡qué vulgo,
> Dios mío! De cara... psh; soy insignificante; de cuerpo,
> no digamos; y, aunque algo valiera, ¿cómo habría de lucir
> mal vestida, con pingos aprovechados, compuestos y vuel-
> tos del revés? Luego soy ignorantísima; no sé nada, no
> hablo más que tonterías y vaciedades, no tengo salero
> ninguno. Soy una calabaza con boca, ojos y manos. ¡Qué
> pánfila soy, Dios mío, y qué sosaina! ¿Para qué nací así?
> (183; 595b)

Abelarda is thus doubly vulnerable when Víctor amuses
himself by befuddling her with half-digested romantic clichés,
presenting himself as the turbulent, restless victim of a fatal
passion. For him, it is a game, but for Abelarda, it is deadly
serious. Far from realizing the truth about his squalid affair, she
invests her unknown 'rival' with a beauty and distinction which she
does not possess. And when Víctor, meeting her on the stairs
one evening, carries the game to the point of embracing her
with feigned ardour, she is genuinely ready to elope with him
immediately.

It is not surprising, then, that when Abelarda realizes, as she does the next day in the interview in the church, that Víctor has been toying with her, and has not the slightest intention of eloping, she is temporarily thrown off balance. The fury of the woman scorned cannot, of course, be directed openly at its principal object, so by a natural process of displacement, it comes to settle on Víctor's son Luisito. That night the boy is restless and peevish, and Abelarda feels an overwhelming conviction that he is the cause of all her ills, and that she will only find peace if she kills him. Then she suddenly remembers that she is not the first person in the family to react in this way:

> Ya no pudo ella dominarse, y saltó del lecho... Quedóse a su orilla inmovilizada, no por la piedad, sino por un recuerdo que hirió su mente con vívida luz. Lo mismo que ella hacía en aquel instante, lo había hecho su difunta hermana en una noche triste... Y Abelarda repetía las mismas palabras de la muerta, diciendo que el pobre niño era un monstruo, un aborto del infierno, venido a la tierra para castigo y condenación de la familia.
>
> Llevóla este recuerdo a comparar la semejanza de causas con la semejanza de efectos, y pensó angustiadísima: '¿Estaré yo loca, como mi hermana?... ¿Es locura, Dios mío?' (322; 649a)

The real significance of romantic cliché in the novel now becomes clear. Víctor's facile talk about *fatalidad* and other such concepts is heinous, not because such things do not exist, but because he is trivializing large and weighty matters. He can talk lightly about shooting himself if his ambitions are frustrated, but Don Ramón actually does so. The notion of a fatal destiny acquires a stark and horrifying reality when we see Abelarda re-enacting, almost like an automaton, her sister's last hours. Furthermore, the impression of fatalism is heightened by the fact that Abelarda's actions are themselves a cliché in a more profound sense than Víctor's second-hand *topoi:* while her behaviour, at one level, stems from irresistible spontaneous feelings, it still conforms to a pre-existing model.

The inevitability of expressing oneself in a hackneyed manner thus becomes in turn part of the destiny of the characters. We

have already seen one example of this in the comparison of
Villaamil's appearance to that of St Bartholomew in the Ribera
painting. Abelarda, too, falls into the same pattern. The previous
night, after Víctor's embrace, she lies awake waiting for him to
come home, so that, as she thinks, they can finally open their
hearts to each other and decide on their future. He, for his
part, has forgotten about the incident on the stairs. As the hours
pass, Abelarda's mind becomes filled with highly dramatic
explanations for his absence, mostly culled from what she has
witnessed in romantic operas:

> Luego pensaba... que la elegantona de las cartas corona-
> das, al enterarse aquella misma noche de que el amante se
> le iba, o al oír de su propio labio tristes acentos de rup-
> tura, tramaba contra él horrible venganza, le convidaba
> a cenar y le envenenaba, echándole en una copa de jerez
> el veneno de los Borgias. Con las extrañas cavilaciones
> mezclaba la sosa mil lances que había visto en las óperas,
> las conjuraciones que arma la mezzo-soprano contra el
> tenor, porque éste la desprecia por la tiple; las perrerías
> del barítono para deshacerse de su aborrecido rival, la
> constancia sublime del tenor... que sucumbiendo a las com-
> binadas artimañas del bajo y la contralto, revienta en
> brazos de la tiple, y concluyen ambos diciéndose que se
> amarán en el otro mundo. (310; 644a-b)

The reference to opera makes it possible to extend the ideas
suggested by the relationship between Abelarda and Víctor to
society at large, for opera is above all a social art form, minis-
tering to the expectations and escapism not only of the *Miaus*,
but of the public which nightly occupies the seats in the Teatro
Real. The romantic clichés which fall from Víctor's lips are not
invented by him, but culled from popular literature, which, like
opera, is also a social institution. He himself, indeed, might
almost be said to be a walking romantic cliché. It is because he
corresponds to accepted stereotypes of elegance and distinction
that he is able to cut such a dash in the mediocre provincial
town where he first meets the Villaamil family. Luisa's infatuation
with him is explicitly referred back to a literary model, being

compared to that of Juliet for Romeo. As we have seen, Abelarda's feelings for him develop along very similar lines, though there is much more explicit emphasis on how she perceives him as the fulfilment of all her assumptions about the alleged refinement of superior people. And Abelarda's infatuation is later grotesquely parodied by Víctor's *momia*, as Argüelles dubs his ageing mistress.

All this confers a very wide frame of reference on the Abelarda-Víctor relationship, a point which has been largely overlooked by critics. Only Roy Jones and Geraldine Scanlon have made a serious attempt to determine the function of this relationship within the context of the novel as a whole, but they refer it only to the inhumanity of the State. The Abelarda-Víctor story, they argue, parallels Villaamil's point by point: thus as the State plays cat and mouse with Don Ramón's hopes, so Víctor with Abelarda's, for his own sadistic pleasure:

> Both Abelarda and Villaamil oscillate between extremes of emotion as their hopes are alternately raised and dashed. Both turn to God for consolation and help and then accuse him of having abandoned them. When the vanity of their hopes becomes obvious their reactions are strikingly similar: frustration drives them insane (although Abelarda only temporarily so), filling them with a desire for destruction and a hatred of order. (*12*, 59)

These points are undoubtedly valid, but the cat-and-mouse element is not the only, or even the most important, feature of the analogy between the two stories. The real significance of the parallel is that both Abelarda and Don Ramón are led by circumstances and their own limited vision into a situation where they can only view their experience in terms of stereotypes, and are consequently more prone to wasting their lives in the pursuit of trivial and unworthy objectives. Moreover, the clichés in which these characters think are part of their entire cultural inheritance, which they share with their contemporaries. Despite the profound temperamental differences between Abelarda, Víctor and Don Ramón, they are part of a continuum which ultimately embraces the whole of Restoration Spain.

The presentation of the Abelarda-Víctor relationship, then, is part of Galdós's strategy for revealing to us a whole society engaged in 'jugando con los sentimientos serios y profundos'. Romantic *topoi* seem to provide society with a ready-made instrument for understanding human relations, but distract attention from the reality of human experience as it actually is. We have already seen how the notion of fatal destiny acquires particular relevance to Abelarda's life when she is driven to try to kill Luis. There is, however, a more low-key kind of *fatalidad* which usually escapes people's attention, but which is, if anything, more interesting and potentially tragic than the obvious and melodramatic forms of suffering. Abelarda's consciousness of the mediocrity of her everyday life turns into a conviction that she is imprisoned permanently within a circle of *cursilería:*

> Las cursis nacen, y no hay fuerza humana que les quite el sello. Nací de esta manera y así moriré. Seré mujer de otro cursi y tendré hijos cursis, a quienes el mundo llamará los *michitos...* (Pausa.) ¿Y cuándo colocarán a Papá? Si lo miro bien, no me importa; lo mismo da. Con destino y sin destino, siempre estamos igual. Poco más o menos, mi casa ha estado toda la vida como está ahora. Mamá no tiene gobierno; ni lo tiene mi tía, ni lo tengo yo. Si colocan a papá, me alegraré por él, para que tenga en qué ocuparse y se distraiga; pero por la cuestión de bienestar, me figuro que nunca saldremos de ahogos, farsas y pingajos... ¡Pobres *Miaus!* (202; 602a)

The 'pequeñez' of Galdós's world is far from trivial, as Unamuno claimed. In *Miau*, it comes to have its own peculiar brand of low-key horror, for the efforts of characters to escape from the circle of 'pequeñez' drive them into cliché, and when the alternatives they seek are seen to be illusory, the vicious circle of drudgery draws tighter. When Ponce, comforting Abelarda after her second bout of madness, says that he would like their wedding day to come quickly, she replies: 'pero todo llega... Detrás de un día viene otro... Todos los días son enteramente iguales' (373; 667b). Limited as Abelarda's intelligence and experience of the world may be, she has shown sufficient sensitivity and capacity for introspection, and for what Galdós calls 'sentimientos más humanos' (205; 603b), for us to appreciate the full grievous import of this remark.

Toying with weighty issues extends even to the area of religion, and it is to this that we must now turn.

CHAPTER V

Luisito

> ... juguetes y chirimbolos sacro-
> recreativos (*Miau*, Chapter 41).

IN a novel devoted to the realistic portrayal of the daily round, it is rather remarkable that so much space is devoted to Luisito's mysterious visions of 'God'. The contrast, or apparent contrast, between the prosaic and ironic style of most of the novel and the supernatural overtones of the 'visions' has led many critics to assume that Luis has a prophetic role in the novel (*1*, 96; *3*, 174; *17*, 30-2). Certainly, unlike the adults, who display varying degrees of imperfection and inconsistency, Luis embodies a refreshing innocence and spontaneity. It is also true that in the presentation of Luis, Galdós has shown his very considerable talent for psychologically accurate treatment of the child's way of looking at the world. It does not necessarily follow, however, that because the description of Luis's perception is authentic and convincing we need to take the content of his perception at its face value. As we shall see, Luis's understanding of his experience is shown to be as relative and limited as that of any other character, and is not wholly free of the influence of cliché.

It is useful to consider first why Luis has these 'visions' at all, for if a rational explanation can be found, the case for regarding Luis as a divine oracle is less strong. Theodore A. Sackett points out that 'Luisito's dreams reflect virtually nothing more than the concrete realities of actions experienced by him and *observed by the reader*' (*17*, 30, emphasis in original). Some of the evidence which Sackett adduces in support of this position is based on a misreading of the text: for example, in arguing that Galdós ensures that Luis overhears the first part of Villaamil's monologue in Chapter 4, beginning, 'Esto ya es demasiado, Señor Todopoderoso', he overlooks the fact that by this stage the boy has already fallen asleep over his homework. But these inaccuracies of detail do not invalidate Sackett's basic point: Galdós is concerned to show that the conversations with 'God' arise naturally from Luis's waking experience.

Sackett is also right to stress that these interludes are dreams rather than hallucinations or supernatural visions. On each occasion, Luis is asleep, either in bed or as the result of one of his periodic black-outs. It is interesting to note, indeed, that in the second version of the manuscript, Galdós suppressed a reference to Luis's having seen the vision when he was awake (460-1). We need not carry the process of rationalization to the extreme of seeking to identify a precise medical cause for these fainting-fits. It is sufficient for our argument that Galdós stresses at several stages in the novel Luis's delicate constitution, and that he gives enough detail about the symptoms which precede the attacks to establish clearly that the cause is physical. More to our purpose is the fact that the 'visions' themselves are skilfully realized pieces of what psychologists call dream-work. That is to say that details from Luis's waking life occur with great vividness in his sleeping consciousness, but are incorporated into the flow of the dream in unexpected ways. Thus after the episode with the cigar-bands in school (Chapter 9), Luis sees 'God' wearing the bands on his fingers like rings. In another dream, 'God' is sitting on one of the chairs from the Villaamils' drawing-room.

Now it is well known that Galdós often used characters' dreams to reveal certain things which their waking consciousness, for one reason or another, did not clearly articulate. But Galdós knew as well as any psychologist that the truth conveyed in a dream is something other than its literal or surface content, something more diffuse and complex. Luis's dreams are no exception. This is why I have deliberately put the name 'God' in inverted commas, for we should be slow to jump to the conclusion that the figure who appears in Luisito's dreams is the God of Christian theology, or that his utterances have a special revelatory value, which is somehow different in kind from the rest of the novel.

In the light of these considerations, let us now look more closely at the dreams themselves. As Sackett has pointed out,

Luisito's 'God' is not omnipotent: he cannot guarantee to do anything to ensure Don Ramón's reinstatement (*17*, 30). It can, of course, be argued that this is not how God works anyway, but the real point, the full implications of which Sackett does not draw out, is that 'God' speaks like an ordinary adult, a parent perhaps, and simply reiterates the conventional judgements of the everyday world. Thus in the first episode, he says gloomily 'Están los tiempos muy malos, muy malos...' (89; 560a). He chides Luis gently for not working harder at his books, but supports him against *Posturitas:* 'Es un ordinario, un mal criado, y ya le restregaré yo una guindilla en la lengua cuando vuelva a decirte *Miau*' (88; 559b). He does urge Luis not to fight back, largely because he is not strong enough rather than as an expression of Christian humility: instead, he should tell the teacher, 'y verás cómo éste pone a *Posturitas* en cruz media hora' (88; 559b).

Nothing in this dialogue suggests a specially lucid or reliable view of reality. The sentiments expressed by 'God' are such as Luis might have heard from any of the adults round him. The conventional nature of these sentiments is corroborated in the second dream, just after Luis's fight with *Posturitas*. 'God' compliments him on having stood up for himself: 'Tuviste razón en enfadarte, y te portaste bien. Veo que eres un valiente y que sabes volver por tu honor' (135; 576b).

Galdós's accurate insight into the nature of dream-work is clearly displayed here, for this is a typical piece of wish-fulfilment. The dream not only enacts 'God's' approval of Luis for fighting *Posturitas*, but also holds out the promise that the schoolmaster will be taken down a peg for his severity: 'El maestro es un bruto, y ya le enseñaré yo a no daros coscorrones tan fuertes' (135; 576b). Dream-work, however, does not consist solely of wish-fulfilment, but often indicates latent anxiety. In the same episode, 'God' takes Luis to task more explicitly for not making progress at his school-work, and links this idea with the problem of his grandfather's unemployment:

> —¿Cómo quieres que yo coloque a tu abuelo si tú no estudias? Ya ves cuán abatido está el pobre señor, esperando como pan bendito su credencial. Se le puede ahogar

con un cabello. Pues tú tienes la culpa, porque si estu-
diaras...

Luis meditó sobre aquello. Su razón hubo de admitir
el argumento, creyéndolo de una lógica irrebatible. Era
claro como el agua: mientras él no estudiase, ¡contro!,
¿cómo habían de colocar a su abuelo? (136; 577a)

But the 'lógica irrebatible' of this is the arbitrary and dis-
jointed logic of a child's dream, not the logic of the waking
world. Those critics who take the 'visions' as a clear and literal
guide to the understanding of the novel have overlooked the
fact that in the everyday world, there can be no possible causal
connexion between Luis's studies and Villaamil's re-employment.
Indeed, the absurdity of seeking any such connexion may be
seen in the novel itself, when Luis tries to put the logic of his
dream into practice during his waking hours. At one stage,
when Luis is recovering from a mild illness, he overhears Doña
Pura say that Villaamil has not been included in a new list of
appointments, on which he had pinned the highest hopes. Galdós
takes the opportunity to warn the reader to interpret Luis's perceptions with some circumspection:

> Estas palabras, impresas en la mente del chiquillo, las rela-
> cionó luego con la cara de ajusticiado del abuelo cuando
> entró a verle. Luis, como niño, asociaba las ideas imper-
> fectamente, pero las asociaba, poniendo siempre entre
> ellas afinidades extrañas sugeridas por su inocencia. (194;
> 599a)

It is this innocence which makes him draw the inference that his
studying harder will somehow help his grandfather to get a job,
and he asks for his books:

> ... lo que admiró a todos, pues no comprendían que quien
> tan poco estudiaba estando bueno, quisiese hacerlo hallán-
> dose encamado. Tanto se impacientó él, que le dieron la
> Gramática y la Aritmética, y las hojeaba, cavilando así:
> 'Ahora no, porque se me va la vista; pero en cuanto yo
> pueda, ¡contro!, me lo aprendo enterito... y veremos enton-
> ces..., ¡veremos!' (198; 600b)

Galdós seems to have wished the reader to pay special attention to this, since he placed it in a position of emphasis at
the end of a chapter. In my view, it is one of the most poignant
episodes in the whole novel, for it shows how even an innocent
child can become a victim of the cycle of imprisonment and
enslavement in which, as we have seen, most of the other characters are enmeshed. Luis's reaction here arises from the inar-
ticulate intuition that he lives in a fundamentally competitive
world, in which everything must be earned by hard work. The
lack of visible connexion between his diligence and its desired
effect is a further variation on the theme of the pursuit of
illusory happiness. That the expression of this theme is here
centred on Luis confers on it something much closer to tragic
quality, and since the novel displays such a tightly-knit structure
of analogy, this tragic quality inevitably affects our feelings
about the other characters.

Luis's dreams are certainly revelatory, but it is going to
unwarranted lengths to regard him as a kind of divine messen-
ger. Sackett calls him 'the voice of truth' (17, 31): it would be
more accurate to say that he is *perceived by Villaamil* as the voice
of truth. This tells us more about Don Ramón than it does
about Luis, and I shall have more to say about this later. As I
have already suggested, Luis's spontaneity and innocence is a
different issue from the accuracy of his perceptions. Indeed,
there are instances in which Luis's reading of the situation is
manifestly inaccurate. In the fourth conversation with 'God' in
Chapter 40, he claims that Abelarda's attempt to strangle him,
and his father's insistence that he should go to live with the
Cabreras, is the fault of a vague personage whom he simply
calls 'el Ministro', repeating, and misapplying, an attribution
which he must have heard many times from his grandfather's
lips. [10] He also claims that Víctor loves Abelarda, but that she
detests him because he told the Minister not to give Villaamil
a job. It is clear that Luis is both judging events from outward

[10] That Galdós thought of Luisito's dreams as made up of parts of his
waking experience is suggested by a passage in Alpha. Under the impact of
the first dream, 'el espíritu seguía viendo aquello que su abuelo llamaba musarañas' (431). 'Musarañas' is the word 'God' uses when he chides Luis for not
concentrating on his school-work.

appearances, and referring everything back to the central issue of his grandfather's unemployment, which has bulked so large in the family's consciousness for so long.

The truth revealed by the 'visions', then, is not to be looked for in the literal meaning of Luis's words or 'God's'. It may justly be claimed, indeed, that this truth is simply the visions themselves: that is, the psychologically authentic picture of a child seeking to understand the adult world. It is, in fact, precisely Luis's appealing simplicity and innocence which leads him to adopt a simple explanation for very complex human problems. But these simple explanations in turn can only be provided by the half-understood frame of reference which he is acquiring from his upbringing. To put the issue in another way, Luis, while too young to understand the adult world fully, is shown in the process of absorbing from his elders the values and assumptions in terms of which he will seek to articulate his experience. He can thus only think of 'God' as punishing those whom Luis would like to see punished (*Posturitas* and the schoolmaster), or giving favours as part of a bargain ('You study and I'll see your grandfather gets a job').

These ideas are reinforced by the third and fourth dream episodes, for by then two important new elements from Luis's waking experience have made their appearance. The first is the death of Paco Ramos, alias *Posturitas*. Far from being the saint that some critics have tried to make him into, it is clear from the way in which Luis reacts to this event that he has all the normal instincts of childhood, which Galdós reminds us at a strategic moment is 'la dichosa edad sin entrañas' (279; 633a). His feelings at the sight of his dying companion are a natural mixture of pity, fear and the desire for self-preservation. As he and his school friends leave the sick boy's house, they come on two of *Posturitas*'s little brothers playing noisily. One of Luis's friends, Silvestre Murillo,

... echándoselas de persona, les reprendió por la bulla que armaban, estando el hermanito malo. Ellos se miraron estupefactos. No comprendían jota. El más pequeño sacó del bolsillo del delantal un pedazo de pan ya muy lamido, todo lleno de babas, y le metió el diente con fe. (258; 624a)

Luis is not as indifferent to Paco's plight as these two are, but the careful placing of this detail just at this point serves to remind us of the general character of children's reactions to these events. We are therefore less surprised to find that Luis's pity for *Posturitas* is further mitigated by resentment at the fact that it was Paco's mother who invented the nickname *Miau*. The conventional view of God as one who punishes provides Luis with a convenient means of assuaging his feelings: 'ahora Dios la castiga de firme por poner motes' (259; 624b). And a closely-related thought swims into his mind even in the midst of the trauma of Paco's funeral:

En medio de aquel inmenso trastorno de su alma, que Luis no podía definir, ignorando si era pena o temor, hizo el chico una observación que se abría paso entre sus sentimientos, como voz del egoísmo, más categórico en la infancia que la piedad. 'Ahora — pensó — no me llamará *Miau*'. (286; 635b)

The integration of the third dream episode into the flow of the narrative is a good example of how smoothly and naturally Galdós can blend several themes together. When Luis falls asleep in the waiting-room of the Congreso, he is still wearing the smart clothes in which he had been fitted out for Paco's funeral. He has gone to the parliament buildings to deliver a letter from his grandfather, who is now pinning his hopes on the patronage of one of the Deputies. On his way to the funeral, Luis has met his aunt Quintina Cabrera, and this brings to the forefront of his consciousness the second of the two elements I mentioned earlier. For Quintina and her husband carry on a lucrative, and largely illegal trade in religious statuary, Mass vessels and vestments. Quintina, being childless, is very keen that Luis should go to live with them rather than with the Villaamils, and on this occasion she tries to interest Luis in the idea by telling him that he can play at saying Mass:

... ahora estamos esperando cálices chiquititos, custodias
que son una monada, casullas así..., para que los niños
buenos jueguen a las misas; santos de este tamaño, así,
mira, como los soldados de plomo, y la mar de candeleri-
tos y arañitas que se encienden en los altares de juguete.
Todo lo tienes que ver, y si vas a la casa, puedes hacer
con ello lo que quieras, pues es para tu diversión. ¿Irás,
rico mío? (285; 635a)

While it is important to what follows in the dream that
these elements should be impressed vividly on Luisito's mind
at this juncture, it is not the first time he has encountered them.
In Chapter 14, we are told that Luis has occasionally visited the
Cabreras' house, and amused himself looking at the stocks of
religious pictures they keep there. One of these is a typical representation of God the Father, holding a blue globe in his hand.
Now Galdós is careful not to commit himself to the view that
Luis's 'visions' are to be explained solely by his contact with
religious art ('¿Se derivaba de esto el fenómeno extrañísimo de
sus visiones? Nadie lo sabe; nadie quizás lo sabrá nunca', 177;
593a). By the same token, however, the suggestion is not totally
discounted. The reason for Galdós's apparent hesitation is probably that he did not wish the reader to attribute Luis's dreams
unequivocally to a single cause: as we have seen, other elements
from his waking consciousness intervene. The fact remains that
the specifically visual aspects of the dreams are derived from
popular religious art. The detail of the blue globe is mentioned
by 'God' in the fourth dream.

The memory-traces of *Posturitas*'s funeral and the meeting
with Quintina combine in the Congreso episode to produce a
vision of 'God' surrounded by chubby cherubs with wings, one
of whom turns out to be Paco Ramos. Significantly, it is precisely
this popular pictorial element which convinces Luis that the
figure in his vision really is God: '... ya no pudo dudar que
aquél era verdaderamente Dios, puesto que tenía ángeles' (295;
638b). In other words, Luis can conceive of God only in terms
of popular images of God. In much the same way, he cannot
imagine a future existence for *Posturitas* which is essentially different from his earthly one. Instead of the mutual forgiveness

which attends a truly Christian experience of death, we find that the relations of Luis and Paco are no different from what they have been in life. The episode ends with an amusing description of Paco making Luis fly into a rage by sticking out his tongue and uttering a final long echoing *Miau*. It is entirely consistent that in the fourth dream-episode, 'God' should tell Luis that he has spanked *Posturitas* and the other cherubs and kept them confined for the rest of the day because they threw his blue globe into the sea; consistent, too, that Luis should represent 'God' as unable to answer his insistent questions about where the cherubs are confined, since neither his waking experience nor the popular images he has inherited provide grounds for an answer.

It is perhaps worth re-emphasizing at this stage that none of the foregoing argument is intended to suggest any criticism of Luis. As I remarked earlier, he retains all the freshness and spontaneity of the child's vision of the world, however much this vision may be limited and conditioned by factors outside himself. This conditioning is the inevitable result of his upbringing, and ultimately of the cultural inheritance of the society to which he belongs, so apportionment of blame to any character or group of characters is irrelevant. It is nonetheless precisely *how* he is influenced by conventional religious thinking which points to the really crucial aspect of Luis's role, which is to reveal something about the adult world, namely the wholesale trivialization of religion. Luis's experience is revelatory, not in any special prophetic sense, but by virtue of the general pattern of analogy of which it forms part.

The similarities between Luis's understanding of religion and that displayed by some of the adult characters underlines not only how far he has been conditioned by popular assumptions, but also how immature these assumptions are. A God who smacks his cherubs or keeps a rod in pickle for over-strict schoolmasters is acceptable to the mature reader as part of a child's moral scheme, but when similar views are expressed by some of the adult characters, the effect is to make them appear not child-like, but childish. Doubtless some of the adult characters' remarks about God are purely conversational, and hardly bear much analysis. But when Doña Pura counters one of Villaamil's expressions of studied pessimism with the remark, 'Eso también es ponerle a Dios cara de palo. Se podría enojar y con muchísima razón' (125; 573a), there are grounds for wondering whether she is not at one with Luis in re-making God in her own image and likeness.

This pattern of analogy emerges more clearly in Chapter 23. Abelarda, in distress and confusion at the course of her relationship with Víctor, has taken to frequenting church, 'ansiosa de corroborar su espíritu en la religión'. It is made clear immediately that 'religion' in this context means external devotional practices. True, Abelarda is sincere enough in her search for spiritual comfort, but Galdós contrives to raise doubts as to whether institutional religion as conventionally understood can provide this consolation, and these doubts are amply confirmed by Abelarda's later lapse into hatred and insanity. Thus, in the chapter in question, the emphasis falls on the visible and material aspects of devotional practice:

> Abelarda... se consolaba mirando los altares, el sagrario donde el propio Dios está guardado, oyendo devotamente la misa, contemplando los santos y vírgenes con sus ahuecadas vestiduras. (244; 618a)

These external and plastic elements are further underlined by the implied parallel between church and theatre hinted at in the statement that Abelarda and Ponce discuss the preacher 'como la noche antes, en la tertulia, hablaban de los cantantes del Real' (245; 618b). Ponce, indeed, subscribes fully to the conventional religion of outward forms, for he is 'uno de los chicos más católicos de la generación presente (aunque más de pico que de obras, como suele suceder)' (244; 618b).

Galdós clearly wishes us to connect Abelarda's religious scheme of values with Luis's, for a great deal of the chapter is taken up with the description of how Luis accompanies Abelarda on her daily visits to church, and the impression that these visits make on the child's mind. By making Luis's uncomplicated perception the centre from which the various religious practices are observed, Galdós can highlight even more strongly the external and material dimension of these practices, with their dependence on devotional bric-à-brac of all kinds:

> A Monserrat encontrábalo frío y desnudo; los santos estaban mal trajeados; el culto le parecía pobre, y además de esto había en la capilla de la derecha, conforme entramos, un Cristo grande, moreno, lleno de manchurrones de sangre, con enaguas y una melena natural tan largo como el pelo de una mujer, la cual efigie le causaba tanto miedo que nunca se atrevía a mirarla sino a distancia, y ni que le dieran lo que le dieran entraba en su capilla. (245; 618b)

Just as there is a mixture of seriousness and irony in the presentation of Abelarda's new-found religious zeal, so it is with Luis. The *Cristo de las melenas* is, to his mind, not at all to be taken lightly. The reader, however, while aware of this fact, can simultaneously grasp the associations of effeminacy suggested by 'enaguas' and 'tan largo como el pelo de una mujer', and the whole tone of the passage is further lightened by the substitution of the colloquial 'entraba' for 'entraría'. This provides a smooth transition to a more explicit equation of religious practice with game-playing. Luis's school-friend Silvestre Murillo is the son of the sexton of Monserrat, and when Abelarda is at her devotions, he often takes Luis into the vestry and shows him the various objects used in public worship,

> ... metiéndose en unas erudiciones litúrgicas que tenían que oír. 'La hostia, verbigracia, lleva dentro a Dios, y por eso los curas, antes de cogerla se lavan las manos para no ensuciarla, y *dominus vobisco* es lo mismo que decir: *cuidado, que seáis buenos*' ... Pero no pudo Murillito hacerle entrar en la capilla del Cristo de las melenas, ni aun asegurándole que él las había tenido en la mano cuando su madre se las peinaba, y que aquel Señor era muy bueno y hacía la mar de milagros. (246-7; 619a-b)

This is as good an example as one is likely to find of how difficult it is to distinguish between a child's view of religion and popular superstitions. Silvestre's view is entirely natural coming from someone of his age, but his notions are not fundamentally different from those of the adults from whom he has presumably acquired his outlook. The entire cultic apparatus of Monserrat and the other Madrid churches is sustained by adults, and exists to minister to their expectations and desires. The theatrical rituals of Monserrat, Quintina's commerce in religious objects, and the images of 'God' reflected in Luis's dreams, all form part of the same social and cultural continuum.

The complex tissue of analogy and association is sustained in the remainder of the chapter. Luisito's growing familiarity with things religious awakens the desire to become a priest, but he can hardly be expected to have much understanding of what this really entails. He wants to be a priest in the same way as any nine-year-old would want to be a fireman after his first visit to a fire-station. Víctor uses this as a spring-board for continuing his cat-and-mouse game with Abelarda, trying to make her believe that her influence has awakened in him the desire for faith. It is worth quoting at some length from this dialogue, to illustrate how Galdós associates religious and romantic clichés in such a way as to suggest that virtually all manifestations of life are cast in theatrical moulds:

> Encontrábase la señorita de Villaamil con fuerzas para tratar aquel asunto, porque la religión se las diera hasta para confesar su secreto a quien no debía oírlo de sus labios.
>
> —Yo quise creer y creí —dijo—. Yo busqué un alivio en Dios, y lo encontré. ¿Quieres que te cuente cómo?
>
> Víctor, que sentado junto a la mesa se oprimía la cabeza entre las manos, levantóse de pronto, diciendo con el tono y gesto de un consumado histrión:
>
> —No hables; me atormentarías sin consolarme. Soy un réprobo, un condenado...
>
> Estas frases de relumbrón, espigadas sin criterio en diferentes libros, las traía muy preparaditas para espetarlas en la primera ocasión. Apenas dichas, acordóse de que había quedado en juntarse en el café con varios amigos, y buscó la fórmula para cortar la hebra que su cuñada había empezado a tender entre boca y boca.
>
> —Abelarda, necesito alejarme, porque si estoy aquí un minuto más... Voy a dar vueltas por las calles, sin dirección

> fija, errante, calenturiento, pensando en lo que no puede
> ser para mí..., al menos todavía... (248; 620a)

It is in the light of the overall development of this part of
the novel that we must interpret Villaamil's reaction, at the end
of this same chapter, to Luis's suggestion that if he prays a lot,
God will give him his job back. Knowing what we do about
how Luis acquired his religious ideas, it is difficult to regard
him as a divine oracle. The real issue is that he is perceived by
the adult members of his family as a divine oracle: his statement

> ... se comentó y repitió hasta la saciedad, celebrándola
> como gracia inapreciable, o como uno de esos rasgos de
> sabiduría que de la mente divina pueden descender a la
> de los seres cuyo estado de gracia les comunica directa-
> mente con aquélla. (250; 620b-621a)

The context makes it clear that Galdós is not committing himself
to the view that Luis's remark really is a 'rasgo de sabiduría'.
It is, indeed, celebrated as such precisely because he is simply
repeating, in all innocence, something he has learned from his
observation of the religious behavior of the adults round him.
That Villaamil should react as he does, almost breaking down
in tears, implies a comment on the old man's immaturity and
lack of perception, which, as we have seen in other respects,
makes him attach a high value to clichés.

This incident provides us with a perspective from which
to judge the religious assiduity which Don Ramón evinces at
a later stage in the novel. At one level, it is natural enough
for Don Ramón in his despair to turn to prayer, but as always
we must pay close attention to context and tone. In the first
place, we are reminded in Chapter 29 that Villaamil has to
make a considerable effort to overcome his inherent pessimism
and have trust in God. Who knows? says Galdós in a characteristically non-committal way, perhaps Villaamil did manage
to reconcile his pessimism with Christian faith. Or perhaps

> ... se proponía aguardar con ánimo estoico el divino fallo,
> renunciando a la previsión de los acontecimientos, resabio
> pecador del orgullo del hombre. (299; 640a)

Without appearing to take sides, Galdós has skilfully suggested that this is what Villaamil ought to be doing, and by implication, both his prayers and his cultivation of despair are shown as a presumptuous attempt to influence the future course of events. There is certainly more than a *resabio de orgullo* in the prayer which follows at the beginning of Chapter 30, which Galdós calls 'mezcla absurda de piedad y burocracia':

Jamás hice ni consentí un chanchullo, jamás, Señor, jamás. Eso bien lo sabes tú, Señor... Ahí están mis libros cuando fui tenedor de la Intervención... Ni un asiento mal hecho, ni una raspadura... ¿Por qué tanta injusticia en estos jeringados gobiernos? Si es verdad que a todos nos das el pan de cada día, ¿por qué a mí me lo niegas? Y digo más: si el Estado debe favorecer a todos por igual, ¿por qué a mí me abandona?... ¡A mí, que le he servido con tanta lealtad! Señor, que no me engañe ahora... Yo te prometo no dudar de tu misericordia como he dudado otras veces; yo te prometo no ser pesimista, y esperar, esperar, en ti. Ahora, Padre nuestro, tócale en el corazón a ese cansado ministro, que es una buena persona: sólo que me le marean con tantas cartas y recomendaciones. (301-2; 640b)

As in Chapter 23, Galdós skilfully brings together several sets of religious attitudes in this episode. A few minutes later, Don Ramón is joined by Luis, who is accompanying Abelarda. He asks the old man whether he has been praying to get his job back, and Villaamil is once again moved to tears. Luis then says that he too prays for the same thing, but so far without result. Then he adds, quite naturally, 'Hoy me he sabido la lección'. Now no-one in the family shows much interest in Luis's studies, and he has told no-one about his dreams, so this is clearly a signal to the reader, reminding him of the whole set of associations surrounding Luis's 'visions', and underlining yet again the parallel between child and adults in their way of thinking about 'God'.

Abelarda, who has been praying in a side chapel, now appears. When Villaamil extols the value of prayer as a balm for the soul, Abelarda is prompted to unburden herself, and blurts out that she is very unhappy. This surprises Don Ramón, 'porque para él no había en la familia más que una desgracia, la cesantía y angustiosa tardanza de la credencial' (304; 641b). Both characters, indeed, are so wrapped up in their own preoccupations that despite the pious atmosphere of the church, which has called forth the exchange of confidences in the first place, neither understands the other. When Abelarda finds she is making no headway with her father, her religious unction gives way to sudden anger, and to mortify the old man, she suddenly gives him the news of Víctor's re-appointment and promotion. This is a shattering blow, and its effect is to banish Villaamil's religious sentiment completely:

> —... Dios no protege más que a los pillos... ¿Crees que espero algo del Ministro ni de Dios? Todos son lo mismo... ¡Arriba y abajo farsa, favoritismo, polaquería! Ya ves lo que sacamos de tanta humillación y de tanto rezo. (306; 642b)

Don Ramón eventually leaves the church, 'sin hacer genuflexión alguna, sin mirar para el altar ni acordarse de que estaba en lugar sagrado' (307; 643a). But not before another issue has been reintroduced into the reader's consciousness. When Abelarda begins to defend Víctor, Villaamil is suddenly struck by the thought that perhaps there is more in this relationship than he had supposed:

> Comparó rápidamente ciertas actitudes de su hija, antes inexplicables, con lo que en aquel momento oía; ató cabos, recordó palabras, gestos, incidentes, y concluyó por declararse que estaba en presencia de un hecho muy grave. Tan grave era y tan contrario a sus sentimientos, que le daba terror cerciorarse de él. Más bien quería olvidarlo o fingirse que era vana cavilación sin fundamento razonable. (306-7; 642b-643a)

There can hardly be a clearer indication of Villaamil's general ineffectualness than that last sentence. I have dwelt at some length on this scene because it is crucial to the understanding of Villaamil's suicide, and to the dénouement of the novel in general. It is indeed in this very chapter, when the three are returning from church, that Víctor embraces Abelarda, an event which has such dramatic consequences later, leading as it does to her attack on Luis.

Víctor uses this attack as a pretext for removing Luis from the Villaamil household, but the real reason has more to do with his financial interest. The Cabreras have agreed not to pursue him for certain legal costs arising from a disputed inheritance if he will let them foster Luis. This is only one of several instances in the closing stages of the novel where the apparent motivation of a character's actions is different from the true one. Doña Pura, for example, misleads Ponce by telling him that Abelarda's hysteria is due to Víctor's wrenching Luis away from them.

A similar contrast exists in the case of Villaamil. Critics have been misled into thinking that Villaamil acts energetically and decisively in the closing stages of the novel, arranging for Luis's future, and waiting until Abelarda's marriage is finally settled before doing away with himself. This interpretation overlooks several points. The ineffectualness which Don Ramón displayed in the Monserrat scene in Chapter 30 is confirmed when he shows no interest at all in the arrangements for the wedding, not even in the inheritance from Ponce's uncle which will enable the couple to live comfortably. True, he does try to expel Víctor fron the house, suspecting rightly that his son-in-law is responsible for Abelarda's erratic behaviour, but this only precipitates Víctor's decision to remove Luis. Although Don Ramón firmly opposes the women's attempts to frustrate Víctor's plan, and although he himself may believe that he is acting decisively in making suitable dispositions prior to his suicide, it is clear to the reader, in the light of what he knows about Víctor's financial circumstances, that the Villaamils will, in any case, eventually have to bow to the inevitable. Don Ramón, indeed, impresses on the women that they have no choice but to part with Luis, since Víctor has the law on his side. The presentation of Don Ramón's reaction to Víctor's decision is surrounded by the hackneyed and grotesque associations which have attended his characterization throughout the novel:

Villaamil dio unas vueltas sobre sí mismo, como si le hiciera girar el vórtice de un ciclón interior, y, después de parar en firme, abrióse de piernas, alzó los brazos enormes, simulando la figura de San Andrés clavado en las aspas, y rugió con toda la fuerza de sus pulmones:

—¡Que se lo lleve..., que se lo lleve con mil demonios! Mujeres locas, mujeres cobardes, ¿no sabéis que *Morimos... Inmolados... Al... Ultraje?* (367; 666a)

It may justifiably be urged here that Villaamil is unbalanced, but as I have argued in Chapter III, his madness and suicide are only the intensification of those obsessional characteristics which have been clearly in evidence throughout the novel. The corollary of his obsession with the State is ineffectualness in the personal and family sphere, and his suicide may be seen as the final abdication of responsibility. It is a mistake to suppose that Don Ramón kills himself in response to a special divine revelation mediated through Luis. The decision to commit suicide is well established by the end of Chapter 37. His resolve wavers, however, when he is conducting Luis to Quintina's house, and he begins to feel remorse at the tall stories he has told about the sacred toys Luis will be able to play with. When Luis reveals his 'visions' and tells him he will find happiness only in heaven, Villaamil's hesitations vanish.

The interpretation of Luis's fourth dream thus assumes particular importance, for we can share Don Ramón's convictions about the wisdom of Luis's advice only if the presentation of 'God's' words gives us grounds for accepting them as reliable. In fact, a close reading of the fourth dream shows that it is just as full of religious clichés as the previous three. There are other indications, too, that Galdós wants us to maintain a circumspect attitude, for it is here that the basic errors of fact in Luis's interpretation of his experience are most clearly to the fore: as we saw earlier, he blames the recent dramatic upheaval in his home on the Minister, and misunderstands the true reasons for Abelarda's fit of madness. There are, besides, more explicit references than before to the way in which Luis has been conditioned by his religious education. Thus the idea that true happiness is to be found in the next life is clearly shown to be a *topos* derived from the sermons Luis has heard in church. When Luis shows reluctance to accept the idea of his grandfather's death, 'God' replies,

> —... Pero, ¿qué es eso?... ¿Pues no dices que vas a ser cura y a consagrarte a mí? Si así lo piensas, vete acostumbrando a estas ideas. ¿No te acuerdas ya de lo que dice el Catecismo? Apréndetelo bien. El mundo ese es un valle de lágrimas, y mientras más pronto salís de él, mejor. Todas estas cosas, y otras que irás aprendiendo, las has de predicar tú en mi púlpito cuando seas grande, para convertir a los malos. Verás cómo haces llorar a las mujeres, y dirán todas que el padrito *Miau* es un pico de oro. Dime, ¿no estás en ser clérigo y en ir aprendiendo ya unas miajas de misa, un poco de latín y todo lo demás?
>
> —Sí, señor... Murillo me ha enseñado ya muchas cosas: lo que significa *aleluya* y *gloria patri*, y sé cantar lo que se canta cuando alzan, y cómo se ponen las manos al leer los santísimos Evangelios.
>
> —Pues ya sabes mucho. Pero es menester que te apliques. En casa de tu tía Quintina verás todas las cosas que se usan en mi culto. (378-9; 670a)

This passage is a very accomplished tissue of allusions, both to the social and conventional aspects of religion on the one hand, and on the other, to what may be called the play aspect. The mention of the Catechism in this context conjures up the entire picture of all those shallow and immature notions of God which we have already seen expressed in different ways by Doña Pura, Abelarda, and Villaamil. I have already suggested that Luis's intention to be a priest simply reflects a child's experience of novelty. Significantly enough, however, this intention is encouraged by the adults: when Luis is angered by his father's profession of atheism, Doña Pura says,

> —... ¿Verdad que mi niño va a ser eclesiástico, para subir al púlpito a echar sus sermoncitos y decir sus misitas? Entonces estaremos todos hechos unos carcamales, y el día que Luisín cante misa, nos pondremos allí de rodillas para que el clериguito nuevo nos eche la bendición. Y el que

estará más humilde y cayéndosele la baba será este zán-
gano, ¿verdad? Y tú le dirás: 'Papá, ya ves cómo al fin has
llegado a creer'. (281; 633b)

As if to remind us that this sentimental view is that of an adult,
Galdós immediately afterwards slips in a reference to the 'rudo
egoísmo' with which Luis greets his father's offer to buy him
a velocipede. The same note of sentimentality occurs in the
fourth dream, where 'God' is made to use the conventional
language of *beatería:* 'Verás cómo haces llorar a las mujeres, y
dirán todas que el padrito *Miau* es un pico de oro'. The references to Murillo and Quintina remind us not only of the strong
element of play in Luis's understanding of religion, but also
of the analogies between this kind of play and the equally
childish approaches of some adults. The final clinching of this
analogy occurs when Villaamil uses the enticements of religious
game-playing to induce Luis to move to Quintina's house, and
then unquestioningly accepts as a divine revelation what is only
the result of Luis's absorption of that sentimental and shallow
religion which these 'juguetes y chirimbolos sacro-recreativos'
both express and foster.

CHAPTER VI

Miau in Twentieth-Century Perspective

IT has been necessary to deal at some length with Luisito's role and its connexion with the whole presentation of the religious theme, not only because the issues it raises are intrinsically complex and interesting, but also because it is difficult to treat any one feature of Luis's presentation in isolation. As we have seen, Luisito's dreams have implications for our judgement of how the adults understand themselves, and ultimately lead us to reflect on the whole complex of social, cultural and moral values on which people's self-images rest. This is only one instance of how each element in the novel dove-tails with all the others: Villaamil's obsession with re-employment in the State administration, Abelarda's fantasies and the religious values of children and adults alike, constitute a series of variations on the theme of enslavement to cliché. This dense texture of analogy and interconnexion is highly characteristic of most Galdós novels, to the extent that the critic can afford to assume that no element is gratuitous: even quite small details can make a contribution to our understanding of the whole.

Miau may therefore justifiably be regarded as a carefully-wrought literary artefact, and it is in this sense that one may speak of its modernity. In general, it seems fair to say that students of Galdós have been comparatively slow to recognize that it is as meaningful to discuss principles of artistic selection and arrangement in the novel as it is with respect to lyric poetry. David Lodge's *Language of Fiction* (London, 1966) and Gabriel Josipovici's *The World and the Book* (London, 1971) exemplify a distinctively twentieth-century approach to fiction which is, when applied even to a nineteenth-century writer like Galdós, much more illuminating than that of, say, Menéndez y Pelayo, whose critical assumptions, revealed in the following very typical extract, have exercised considerable influence on successive generations of readers:

> La falta de selección en los elementos de la realidad; la prolija acumulación de los detalles; esa selva de novelas que, aisladamente consideradas, suelen no tener principio ni fin, sino que brotan las unas de las otras con enmarañada y prolífica vegetación, indican que el autor procura remedar el oleaje de la vida individual y social y aspira... a la integridad de la representación humana... [11]

If the argument of the foregoing chapters is valid, there are grounds for saying that Galdós is less concerned with imitating the flux of life than with enabling us, as it were, to see behind the surface of this life to the principles that determine it, and to form judgements about the value or otherwise of these principles.

The modernity of *Miau* is also revealed in the way in which it blurs the distinctions between comedy and tragedy. It is, of course, true that the two perspectives had been combined in the literature of earlier periods. But it was only with the romantics that this practice was underpinned by a coherent body of theory, which in turn influenced the development of realism, and the general anti-heroic tone of much modern fiction. However, even if few critics of the novel would subscribe nowadays to the classical doctrine of the separation of styles, it remains true that many academic readers of *Miau* have, as Lambert has pointed out, gone very far off course 'by looking in the novel for something "positive", for a firm foothold in its multi-dimensional irony' (*13*, note 23). The disagreements among the various participants in the controversy over *Miau* stem in large measure from their tendency to suppose that *Miau* must be either a tragic story or a comic satire, that Villaamil is either a martyr or a fool. In attempting to argue that the correct approach to *Miau* is more likely to be both/and, I am far from suggesting that Galdós is guilty of any 'infirmity of purpose'. On the contrary, the comic and grotesque elements in the novel are essential

---

[11] Menéndez y Pelayo-Pereda-Pérez Galdós, *Discursos leídos ante la Real Academia Española en las recepciones públicas del 7 y 21 de febrero de 1897* (Madrid, 1897), pp. 86-7.

to Galdós's overall strategy, and assist in the revelation of the true depth and seriousness of the subject-matter: by detaching the reader from the wrong kind of involvement in the fortunes of the individual characters, and by skilful control of aesthetic distance, Galdós ensures that attention will be directed to those issues which are really important.

This means that the reader is far from being a passive recipient of the message which Galdós wishes to communicate. One of the most persistent commonplaces of modern novel criticism is the notion that the nineteenth-century novel is characteristically communicated to the reader in what is known as the omniscient narrative mode. That is to say that the author casts himself in the role of an Olympian god-like figure, manipulating his characters as he pleases, describing what goes on in the most secret recesses of their minds, and telling the reader all he needs to know. The experience of reading such a novel is that of absorbing the content of someone else's thoughts, as a sponge absorbs water. The distinctive feature of the twentieth-century novel, the argument goes on, is that the author lays aside any claim to omniscience, and does not presume to tell the reader what to think. The novel, instead of being received passively by the reader, must be re-created and re-experienced every time it is read, through the active participation of the reader. This generalization is risky, to say the least, but even if it were valid, Galdós would have to be considered an exception to it. Nor is it any less misleading to claim that Galdós's *novelas dialogadas* are a bridge connecting the classical realist mode of his previous work with an objective form which anticipates the developments of our own time. [12] It is perhaps legitimate, given that the first of these experiments, *Realidad* (1889), comes only a year after *Miau*, to look for anticipations of what one may call reader-participation in the earlier novel. But it would be more accurate to say that a non-committal style of narration which demands a high degree of alertness, discrimination and discernment on the part of the reader is well established in Galdós's work by 1882 at the latest, and probably before. No-one who has read *El amigo*

[12] 'Para borrar en el relato la sombra enojosa del narrador omnisciente, el autor canario inventará la novela *hablada* o teatral'. Laureano Bonet, *De Galdós a Robbe-Grillet* (Madrid, 1972), p. 115.

Manso, Tormento or *Lo prohibido,* to mention only three examples, can doubt that Galdós makes the most rigorous demands on the reader's understanding, human sympathy and intelligence.

In these three ways, *Miau* anticipates later developments in the novel, and is well placed to appeal to modern readers. A word of caution should, perhaps, be uttered at this point. We should not exaggerate the modernity of *Miau* to the extent of taking an anachronistic approach. Ricardo Guillón does so when he argues that Villaamil is destroyed by an absurd bureaucratic system which in turn reflects an absurd, Kafkaesque world (*3,* 261ff, especially 266). But modern man is bewildered not only by being imprisoned within vast impersonal systems of relation, but also, and primarily, by the collapse of confidence in traditional moral certainties, a collapse by which the author himself is affected. There is no such despair in the case of Galdós. While he does not explicitly defend any set of standards, moral values are never very far away. In *Miau,* they may be defined as everything which the Villaamil family and their society are not. However close Villaamil and other characters may come to acquiring tragic status, however inevitable their imprisonment in their situation may seem, the satirical tone of the novel clearly implies that in the last analysis things *ought* to be different. The parodying of romantic love, of religion, of devotion to duty implies the existence of a standard of which the *M-I-A-U* world and, by extension, Restoration Spain, falls lamentably short.

The ultimate value of *Miau* for the twentieth-century reader, then, is that it maintains a balance between universality of reference and historical particularity. It is a mistake to suppose, as Casalduero does (*1,* 95), that the presentation of the world of bureaucracy in *Miau* is merely a pretext for the exploration of large existential issues. Equally, however, it would be futile to try to find out from the novel what Galdós really thought about income tax. *Miau* is, in its final essence, the result of a wise and percipient artist's attempt to judge his contemporaries, in their concrete historical and national circumstances, by moral standards which are perennially relevant.

Bibliographical Note

EDITIONS

(See note on References, p. 7). At the time of writing, the Labor edition is out of print. This, while textually reliable, has a rather poor introduction and notes. The edition by Edward R. Mulvihill and Roberto Sánchez (New York, 1970) is still available, but cannot be recommended as it is considerably abridged. Ricardo Gullón's edition (Madrid: Revista de Occidente, 1957), while no longer in print, will be found reliable.

GENERAL STUDIES

1. Joaquín Casalduero, *Vida y obra de Galdós*, 2nd edition (Madrid, 1961). A pioneering study, but rather dated. Structures the critical discussion of novels around an excessively rigid dichotomy between *materia* and *espíritu*.

2. Sherman H. Eoff, *The Novels of Pérez Galdós* (St Louis, 1954). A thorough but plodding study of the development of Galdós's novels from a psychological perspective.

3. Ricardo Gullón, *Galdós, novelista moderno* (Madrid, 1960). Reprints without alteration the long introduction of his 1957 edition (see above). As its title suggests, considers Galdós's work, and especially *Miau*, from an anachronistically modernizing point of view.

4. José F. Montesinos, *Galdós*, 3 vols (Madrid, 1968-72). Written with a refreshing disrespect for received opinion, but while many of its insights are illuminating, they are poorly documented.

BIOGRAPHY

5. H. Chonon Berkowitz, *Pérez Galdós, Spanish Liberal Crusader* (Madison, 1948). The standard biography of Galdós. Usefulness limited, because it does not give sources.

GALDÓS ON THE NOVEL

6. Laureano Bonet, ed., *Benito Pérez Galdós, Ensayos de crítica literaria* (Barcelona, 1972). Contains all the most important essays on the novel by Galdós. Long and perceptive introduction by the editor.

COLLECTIONS OF ARTICLES

7. Leopoldo Alas, *Galdós* (Madrid, 1912). Collected reviews and comments. Sometimes betrays limitations of its journalistic form, but can still be read with profit.

8. D. M. Rogers, ed., *Benito Pérez Galdós* (Madrid, 1973). An uneven collection, but contains some of the best of recent Galdós criticism, as well as important essays by Galdós's contemporaries.

9. *Galdós Studies*, Vol. I, ed. by J. E. Varey (London, 1970); vol. II, ed. by Robert J. Weber (London, 1974). Two important collections of essays, some excellent, by British and American scholars.

10. *Cuadernos Hispanoamericanos*, 250-2 (1970-1). A commemorative number of this journal, containing much dross, but some good articles.

11. *Letras de Deusto*, IV, no. 8 (July-December 1974). A well-balanced and useful collection.

STUDIES OF MIAU

12. R. O. Jones and Geraldine M. Scanlon, '*Miau*: prelude to a reassessment', *Anales Galdosianos*, VI (1971), 53-62. A useful corrective to Weber's unfavourable view of Villaamil.

13. A. F. Lambert, 'Galdós and the anti-bureaucratic tradition', *Bulletin of Hispanic Studies*, LIII (1976), 35-49. An excellent study of the tradition of political criticism as it refers to *cesantes*.

14. A. A. Parker, 'Villaamil: tragic victim or comic failure?', *Anales Galdosianos*, IV (1969), 13-23. Favourable to Villaamil, but overstates the case.

15. H. Ramsden, 'The question of responsibility in Galdós's *Miau*', *Anales Galdosianos*, VI (1971), 63-78. A judicious and carefully-argued refutation of Weber.

16. G. W. Ribbans, 'La figura Villaamil en *Miau*', *Actas del Primer Congreso Internacional de Estudios Galdosianos* (Ediciones del Excmo. Cabildo Insular de Gran Canaria, 1977). A sensitive and balanced study of the relationship between comedy and pathos in Don Ramón's presentation.

17. Theodore A. Sackett, 'The meaning of *Miau*', *Anales Galdosianos*, IV (1969), 25-38. Despite some factual inaccuracies, a judicious and comprehensive view of the novel, one of the few to take account of characters other than Don Ramón.

18. Robert J. Weber, *The Miau Manuscript of Benito Pérez Galdós*, University of California Publications in Modern Philology, vol. 72 (Berkeley and Los Angeles, 1964). A meticulous piece of scholarly textual study, throwing much light on Galdós's creative procedures, but not strong on literary criticism.